A BOX OF
RAIN

A BOX OF

RAIN

ROBERT HUNTER

VIKING

VIKING
Published by the Penguin Group
Viking Penguin, a division of Penguin Books USA Inc.,
375 Hudson Street, New York, New York 10014, U.S.A.
Penguin Books Ltd, 27 Wrights Lane,
London W8 5TZ, England
Penguin Books Australia Ltd, Ringwood,
Victoria, Australia
Penguin Books Canada Ltd, 2801 John Street,
Markham, Ontario, Canada L3R 1B4
Penguin Books (N.Z.) Ltd, 182–190 Wairau Road,
Auckland 10, New Zealand

Penguin Books Ltd, Registered Offices:
Harmondsworth, Middlesex, England

First published in 1990 by Viking Penguin,
a division of Penguin Books USA Inc.

10   9   8   7   6   5   4   3   2   1

LIBRARY OF CONGRESS CATALOGING IN PUBLICATION DATA
Hunter, Robert.
A box of rain : lyrics of Robert Hunter.
p.   cm.
Lyrics of songs performed by the Grateful Dead and others.
Discography: p.
ISBN 0-670-83412-2
1. Popular music—Texts.   I. Grateful Dead (Musical group)
II. Title.
ML54.6.H85B7   1990 [Case]
782.42166'026'8—dc20   90–50040
MN

Printed in the United States of America
Set in Bembo
Designed by Fritz Metsch

PREFACE

This volume contains all my lyrics for the Grateful Dead, the Jerry Garcia solo album material, my personal repertoire, works written for the New Riders, Jefferson Starship, and Dylan, plus lyrics rescued from napkins, notebooks and scraps of yellowing memory.

Aficionados of the work will find a few unsupposed things lurking in familiar lines. Stranger things thought to have been heard may not be found at all. My inclination has been to forgo printing lyrics on the jackets of recordings and let the songs live out their lives in the listener's ear. However, an exact accounting is not a bad idea in case someone has put it together all wrong and is about to make his move . . . or in the event that a congressional committee decides to investigate the Dead for satanic and/or liberal content.

Song lyrics are often embarrassed by print, and some of mine are no exception. Rhyme, rhythm, and manageable phrasing impose restrictions on what might be said; fortunately, once in a while, the very limitations help to create something which could be said no other way.

Alphabetical order was chosen both for easy access and to allow each song to exist in its own right, apart from album or temporal contexts. Suites, such as *Terrapin Station,* which are *designed* to fit together, will be found at the back of the book. Those desiring a chronological reading are invited to consult the discography at the back of this volume.

My versions of these songs are no more "the real ones" than those that may have spoken to some of you through the music darkly twenty years ago. I hope that seeing the intended words will provide you with an interesting, if not always convincing variant on the words some of you *actually* heard.

I dedicate this *Box of Rain* to those who have taken a line or two of it to heart. Believe it if you need it—if you don't, just pass it on.

—Robert Hunter

CONTENTS

NOTE: Titles in *italics* recorded by the Grateful Dead. Titles marked with * appear on solo recordings of Jerry Garcia. Songs marked with ^ appear on my own solo recordings. Titles without markings are unrecorded. Titles marked by a number in parentheses appear on the following albums:
1. Jefferson Starship: *Dragonfly*
2. New Riders of the Purple Sage: *Brujo*
3. Mickey Hart: *Rolling Thunder*
4. Kantner, Slick, Freiberg: *Baron von Tollbooth & the Chrome Nun*
5. Quicksilver Messenger Service: *Solid Silver*
6. Grace Slick: *Manhole*
7. New Riders: *Powerglide*
8. Bob Dylan: *Down in the Groove*

A BOX OF
RAIN

AIM AT THE HEART

Time doesn't fly
Just hangs over like the sky
It's *we* who go by
Makes no difference how or why
    Everything you cherish
    Throws you over in the end
    Thorns will grab your ankles
    From the gardens that you tend
Damned if you do
Double damned if you don't try
Caught on the fly
Hello fades into good-bye

Aim at the heart
Don't ask whose love you're stealing
Aim at the heart
Even when it's too revealing
Aim at the heart
I tell you, aim at the heart

Sitting on a back street many years ago
The tears from your eyes did flow
Feeling out of place inside the time
    when you were born
No place else to go
    Suddenly a rainbow rose
    And spread across the land
    Hung there while the Beatles sang
    I want to hold your hand

What can you say?
Here tomorrow, gone today
Faith fades away
For idols with their feet of clay
    Keep your head upon your neck
    It's not too late for that

Even though the winds of change
    Have blown away your hat
Aim at the heart
I tell you, aim at the heart

Aim at the heart
Don't ask whose love you're stealing
Aim at the heart
Even when it's too revealing
Aim at the heart
I tell you, aim at the heart

Kiss it and pass
Time become a looking glass
Where love combs her hair
Look again, she isn't there
    The echo of her laughter
    Fades into the western skies
    Where ribbons that you bought her
    Are reflected in her eyes

Aim at the heart
Don't ask whose love you're stealing
Aim at the heart
Even when it's too revealing
Aim at the heart
I tell you, aim at the heart

3

ALABAMA GETAWAY

Thirty-two teeth in a jawbone
Alabama cryin' for none
Before I have to hit him
I hope he's got the sense to run

Reason those poor girls love him
Promise them anything
Reason they believe him
He wears a big diamond ring

Alabama getaway
Alabama getaway
Only way to please me
Turn around and leave
and walk away

Majordomo Billy Bojangles
Sit down and have a drink with me
What's this about Alabama
Keeps comin' back to me?

Heard your plea in the courthouse
Jury box began to rock and rise
Forty-nine sister states all had
Alabama in their eyes

Alabama getaway
Alabama getaway
Only way to please me
Turn around and leave
and walk away

Why don't we just give Alabama
rope enough to hang himself?
Ain't no call to worry the jury
His kind takes care of itself

Twenty-third Psalm Majordomo
reserve me a table for three
in the Valley of the Shadow
just you, Alabama and me

Alabama getaway
Alabama getaway
Only way to please me
turn around and leave
and walk away

L'ALHAMBRA

L'Alhambra
Six guitars
Each plays
a different tune

Five play slowly
One plays quick,
an Allegrias
in clear moon

Eight hands clap
to summon up
the Tarantelle—
Beware!

Yo no he bailado
con su hija ya
I have not danced
with your sister yet

Yo no he bailado
con su hija
No he bailado desde
Hay que no baile

L'Alhambra
Five guitars
play as one—
together now

One has gone
into the shadow
Gone with him
is his guitar

Six hands clap
Two are gone now
Captured by
the Tarantelle

Someone else
must play guitar
when time comes
for making love

No he bailado desde
Las Zapatas son perdidas
I have not danced
since my shoes were lost

Yo no he bailado
con su hija ya
No he bailado desde
Hay que no baile

I have not danced
with your sister yet
Is that she who
sleeps by my guitar?

(Written to a Moorish setting composed by Mickey Hart that eventually evolved into a wordless melodic segment of *Terrapin Station*)

ALLIGATOR

Sleepy alligator in the noonday sun
Sleepin' by the river just like he usually done
Call for his whiskey
He can call for his tea
Call all he wanta but he
can't call me

Oh, no
I been there before
and I'm not comin' back around
there no more

Creepy alligator comin' all around the bend
Talkin' 'bout the times when we was mutual friends
I check my mem'ry
I check it quick, yes, I will
I check it runnin'
some old kind of trick

Oh, no, well, I
been there before
and I ain't a-comin' back around
there no more
no, I'm not

Hung up waitin' for a windy day   *(lyrics by Grateful Dead)*
Hung up waitin' for a windy day
Tear down the Fillmore
Gas the Avalon

Ridin' down the river in an old canoe   *(lyrics by Ron McKernan)*
a bunch of bugs and an old tennis shoe
out of the river all ugly and green
the biggest old alligator that I've ever seen
teeth big and pointed and his eyes were buggin' out
contact the union, put the beggars to route

screamin' and yellin' and lickin' his chops
he never runs, he just stumbles and hops
just out of prison on six dollars' bail
mumblin' at bitches and waggin' his tail

Alligator runnin' 'round my door (4x)

Alligator creepin' 'round the corner of my cabin door
He's comin' 'round to bother me some more

(This was the first of my lyrics recorded by the Dead. I got paid two hundred fifty dollars from the record advance for *Anthem of the Sun* with which I bought a used car and headed north to Seattle, where I tried to make a living restringing beads from Goodwill for a friend's boutique. I made about five dollars at this occupation. The car broke down, which was okay, since I couldn't afford gas for it, so I hitchhiked back to S.F. and decided to hang in there with the Dead. Pigpen added lyrics of his own to "Alligator" and I've presented it here with his turns of phrase intact.)

ALTHEA

I told Althea I was feeling lost
Lacking in some direction
Althea told me upon scrutiny
my back might need protection

I told Althea that treachery
was tearing me limb from limb
Althea told me: Now cool down boy—
settle back easy, Jim

You may be Saturday's child all grown
moving with a pinch of grace
You may be a clown in the burying ground
or just another pretty face
You may be the fate of Ophelia
sleeping and perchance to dream—
honest to the point of recklessness
self-centered to the extreme

Ain't nobody messing with you but you
your friends are getting most concerned—

loose with the truth
maybe it's your fire
but baby. . . don't get burned
When the smoke has cleared, she said,
that's what she said to me:
You're gonna want a bed to lay your head
and a little sympathy

There are things you can replace
and others you cannot
The time has come to weigh those things
this space is getting hot—
you know this space is getting hot

I told Althea
I'm a roving sign—
that I was born to be a bachelor—
Althea told me: Okay, that's fine—
So now I'm out trying to catch her

Can't talk to me without talking to you
We're guilty of the same old thing
Talking a lot about less and less
And forgetting the love we bring

ARIEL

The silver fox has shed its tail now
left it by the frozen water
the leaves were drifting down
now they are gone, gone, gone

I draw milady's carriage
ever since her horse retired
I don't think I can pull much longer
I've never been this tired before

Up jump the black chain dancers
empty hands that grasp for answers
fasten on to one another—fly
fly, fly, fly away

Ariel is sweetly singing:
Wait you, just one more season
you're not blind—you only hide your
eyes within your hands
    —within your hands

Ariel—Ariel
A-ri-el . . . Ariel

There is no night like this night
where candles burn through daylight
minds restrained by golden tethers fade
fade, fade, fade away

The sun objects with smiling sadness
Roman highways laced with diamonds
Sink like grave Atlantis into
dreams of other days—they fade away

Monuments to crippled madness
Puppets dangle in the treetops

The cold magician carves his voice in stone
then flies away—then flies away

Ariel sings overhead
Deaf men mouth the words she's said
but they don't hear the songs she's singing now
oh, no—not now

Ariel—Ariel
A-ri-el . . . Ariel

As wild and unholy place
as anyplace I've ever been
you can knock and knock and knock
no one comes to let you in—no one comes

As solid and as fine a floor
as any floor I've walked upon
broke beneath my footsteps
I've got no place left to stand
not anymore

Loves to love and not to chain
some are lost but some remain
nothing can replace the light
that once has died—turned to night—no one
    can

If I had the sense to know
which things count and which are show
I'd hold my fate within my hand
instead of all these chains and bands—yes, I
    would!

Ariel—Ariel
A-ri-el . . . Ariel

(These lyrics, written in 1964, were not recorded until ten years later, when Mickey Hart independently created a musical arrangement that brought them to mind.)

9

ARIZONA LIGHTNING

Arizona Lightning
cut out like a thundershot
his voice rang clear across the U.S.A.
Where other men have tried and failed
ended up their days in jail
this man always knew the horse to play

Pick your bed up, beggar man
bird in the bush and none in the hand—
What's your sad excuse to live so long?
Men been hanged for better things
than half the things you did today
You go find some other place to stay

Arizona thundershower
count the days and kill the hour
Six foot deep don't seem so awful low, you know
When the eagle hits the ground
sparks will fly for miles around
Who could blame a man to curse or pray?

Strike a light or curse the shade
Some of us have got it made
while some men's children got to stall for time
What you get for what you got
still don't leave an awful lot
Could be you've nothing left to give away

California lightning chain
kicked out in the driving rain
you broke every law of God and man
An honest man would stand and die
if he had one good reason why
or even half a leg on which to stand

You don't look like one of me
and I don't think I'm one of you
but on the other hand you got your gun
I don't need to have to ask
what's that face behind your mask?
It ain't much different than any other one I've seen

Alabama backslap—
one step forward and two steps back—
that won't get you back to Buffalo, you know
Just one thing left to say
Every dog will have his day
Take it home but keep your hands off mine

(*lines occurring during the "out"*)

Take your own but keep your hands off mine. . . .
Knock it down but don't write on my wall. . . .
Take it home but leave my own alone. . . .
Bump and grind but keep your hands off mine. . . .

(This song has been called "a whole forest of wild turkeys." I wrote it in Lake Havasu, Arizona [where they have erected the old London Bridge in the desert over a stretch of the Colorado River], while watching the Watergate hearings on TV. Most of the venom is directed at Nixon, but the "Alabama backslap" line refers to Ted Kennedy getting chummy with Governor George Wallace and his Southern votes as the Republican Party appeared ready to crumble.)

ATTICS OF MY LIFE

In the attics of my life
Full of cloudy dreams unreal
Full of tastes no tongue can know
And lights no eye can see
    When there was no ear to hear
    You sang to me

I have spent my life
Seeking all that's still unsung
Bent my ear to hear the tune
And closed my eyes to see
    When there were no strings to play
    You played to me

In the book of love's own dream
Where all the print is blood
Where all the pages are my days
And all my lights grow old
    When I had no wings to fly
    You flew to me

You
flew
to me

In the secret space of dreams
Where I dreaming lay amazed
When the secrets all are told
And the petals all unfold
    When there was no dream of mine
    You dreamed of me

BELIEVE IT OR NOT

One or two moments
a piece of your time
is all I am asking
and I'll give you mine
One or two moments
out of all you have got
to show how I love you
believe it or not

Remember the day
I rolled into town
with my heart in my shoes,
my head hanging down?
Now my only trouble
the rest I forgot
is to show how I love you
believe it or not

Done time in the lockup
Done time in the street
Done time on the upswing
and time in defeat
I know what I'm asking
and I know it's a lot
when I say that I love you
believe it or not

I know I'm no angel
my prospects are high
as the flood line in summer
when the river's gone dry
but I'll roll up my shirt-sleeves
and make my best shot
to show how I love you
believe it or not

Right now while the sun shines
on the crest of the hill
with a breeze in the pines
and a gray whippoorwill
making music together
that guitars never caught
let me show how I love you
believe it or not

(A C&W lyric reminiscent of the kind of stuff I remember hearing coming from tavern jukeboxes in 1948, when my father would stop in to have a few while I waited out in the car.)

BERTHA

I had a hard run
Running from your window
I was all night running, running, running
I wonder if you care?
I had a run-in
Run around and run down
Run around a corner
Run smack into a tree

I had to move
Really had to move
That's why, if you please
I am on my bended knees
Bertha, don't you come around here
    anymore

Dressed myself in green
I went down to the sea
Try to see what's going down
Maybe read between the lines
Had a feeling I was falling, falling, falling

Turned around to see
Heard a voice calling, calling, calling
You was coming after me
Back to me

I had to move
Really had to move
That's why, if you please
I am on my bended knees
Bertha, don't you come around here
    anymore

Ran into a rainstorm
Ducked into a bar door
It was all night pouring, pouring rain
But not a drop on me

Test me, test me
Why don't you arrest me?
Throw me in the jailhouse
Until the sun goes down
Till it go down

I had to move
Really had to move
That's why, if you please
I am on my bended knees
Bertha, don't you come around here
    anymore

BILLBOARD DREAMS

Saw this skinny redhead
On a corner in L.A.
Asked her for the time
If not the minute, then the day
She looked a little cautious
But she didn't run away
That's as close to romance
As I'm looking for today

Billboard Dreams
Stuck in the middle of
Billboard Dreams
Struck by the riddle of
Billboard Dreams
I'm still cryin' for you-oooo

Asked her for a cigarette
And could she spare a light
She said she didn't smoke
Because mama raised her right
She didn't drink or gamble
Or run around at night
Didn't have a fellow
She don't even like to fight

Billboard Dreams. . .etc.

Came to the conclusion
There must be something wrong
Either she's a liar or
I'm living in a song
Invited her to dinner
She said: let it be my treat
That's when I lost my appetite
And crumpled in defeat

Billboard Dreams. . .etc.

Told her I was desperate
I was running from the law
She said I'll give you shelter,
Come home and meet my ma
I tried to edge away
But there was traffic in the street
Knocked me for a somersault
I landed at her feet

I believe that will is free
That fate is in your pants
Nothing written in the stars
It's all a game of chance
Tell it to the jury
'Cause the judge is on parole
Tell it in a hurry
'Cause we really got to roll

Billboard Dreams
Stuck in the middle of
Billboard Dreams
Struck by the riddle of
Billboard Dreams
I'm still cryin' for you-oooo

BIRDSONG   *. . . for Janis*

All I know is something like a bird
within her sang
All I know, she sang a little while
and then flew on

Tell me all that you know
I'll show you
Snow and rain

If you hear that same sweet song again
will you know why?
Anyone who sings a tune so sweet
is passing by

Laugh in the sunshine
sing
cry in the dark
fly
through the night

Don't cry now
Don't you cry
Don't you cry
anymore
la-la-la-la
Sleep
in the stars
don't you cry
dry your eyes
on the wind
la-la-la-la
la . . .

BLACK MUDDY RIVER

When the last rose of summer pricks my finger
And the hot sun chills me to the bone
When I can't hear the song for the singer
And I can't tell my pillow from a stone

I will walk alone by the black muddy river
And sing me a song of my own
I will walk alone by the black muddy river
And sing me a song of my own

When the last bolt of sunshine hits the mountain
And the stars start to splatter in the sky
When the moon splits the southwest horizon
With the scream of an eagle on the fly

I will walk alone by the black muddy river
And listen to the ripples as they moan
I will walk alone by the black muddy river
And sing me a song of my own

Black muddy river
Roll on forever
I don't care how deep or wide
If you got another side
Roll muddy river
Roll muddy river
Black muddy river roll

When it seems like the night will last forever
And there's nothing left to do but count the years
When the strings of my heart start to sever
And stones fall from my eyes instead of tears

I will walk alone by the black muddy river
And dream me a dream of my own
I will walk alone by the black muddy river
And sing me a song of my own
And sing me a song of my own

BLACK PETER

All of my friends come to see me last night
I was laying in my bed and dying
Annie Beauncu from Saint Angel
say, "The weather down here so fine"

Just then the wind
came squalling through the door
but who can
the weather command?
Just want to have
a little peace to die
and a friend or two
I love at hand

Fever roll up to a hundred and five
Roll on up
gonna roll back down
One more day
I find myself alive
tomorrow
maybe go
beneath the ground

See here how everything
lead up to this day
and it's just like
any other day
that's ever been
Sun goin' up
and then the

sun it goin' down
Shine through my window and
my friends they come around
come around
come around

People may know but
the people don't care
that a man could be
as poor as me. . . .
"Take a look at poor Peter
he's lyin' in pain
now let's go run
and see"

Run and see
hey, hey,
run and see

(I wrote this as a brisk piece like Kershaw's "Louisiana Man." Garcia took it seriously, though, dressing it in subtle changes and a mournful tempo. The bridge verse—"See here how everything lead up to this day . . ."—was written after the restructuring of the piece and reflects the additional depth of possibility provided for the song by his treatment.)

BLACK SHAMROCK

Black Shamrock/Cut out the smart talk
If you can't hack it/why don't you walk?
Get away/while it's still a sunny day
Follow through
Remember what you're dreaming of
Dreaming of
Somewhere there's an altitude
bound to match your attitude

Shadowland melody
Three-part harmony
Might as well be you as me
and you can sing on key
Yes, indeed
Remember what you're dreaming of
Dreaming of

Black Shamrock/Hung up in dry dock
Forces in deadlock/you know what you
    know
Fall below/you're a very easy laugher
But you know
Can't laugh at what you're dreaming of
Dreaming of
When it's all said and done
Maybe you should cut and run

Full-speed power dive
Kick it into overdrive
If anyone gets out alive
It might as well be you
Follow through
Remember what you're dreaming of
Dreaming of

Black Shamrock/Shoot off the padlock
This is your own place, you don't have
    to knock
No one's home
You live here on your own
Yeah, you do
Remember what you're dreaming of
Dreaming of

Sterling steel, made to last
Shame the scandals of your past
Stake your claim and mine it fast
You've nothing left to prove
Follow through
Remember what you're dreaming of
Dreaming of

BLUES FOR ALLAH

Arabian wind
The Needle's Eye is thin
The Ships of State sail on mirage
but drown in sand
in No-Man's Land
where ALLAH does command

What good is spilling
blood? It will not
grow a thing

"TASTE ETERNITY"
the sword sings Blues for ALLAH
In'sh'ALLAH

They lie where they fall
There's nothing more to say
The desert stars are bright tonight,
let's meet as friends
The flower of Islam
The fruit of Abraham

The thousand stories have
come 'round to one again
Arabian Night
our gods pursue their fight
What fatal flowers of
darkness spring from
seeds of light

Bird of Paradise—Fly
In white sky
Blues for ALLAH
In'sh'ALLAH

Let's see with our heart
these things our eyes have seen
and know the truth will still lie
somewhere in between

Under eternity
Under eternity
Under eternity
Blue
Bird of Paradise
Fly
In white sky
Under eternity
Blues
for ALLAH
In'sh'ALLAH

(This lyric is a requiem for King Faisal of Saudi Arabia, a progressive and democratically inclined ruler [and, incidentally, a fan of the Grateful Dead] whose assassination in 1975 shocked us personally. The lyrics were printed in Arabic on the jacket of the Middle East release of the album.)

BOLL WEEVIL RAG

Boll Weevil told me
Stay away from my girl
Boll Weevil told me
Stay away from her

Don't call her early in the morning
Or in the evening, too
Boll Weevil said: Stay away
and I'll thank you if you do

I took one look at him
and he took a look at me
I said: What a good party
He said: Yes, indeed

They got hot tamale and the Perry-ay
Havana Tampa, too
I said: I'm gonna get your girl
He said: I'm warning you

Don't make me tell you twice
I don't like to preach
If I catch you with my girl
you're gonna have to reach

I said: I don't take no stick from a weevil
He said: Baby, die!
The party crowd jumped under the rug
He pulled out his knife

While we was circling round and round
his baby doll pulled out
with a bottle fly from Georgia
which made Boll Weevil shout:

I been deceived and I been cheated
What more can I say?
Gimme a Havana Tampa,
hot tamale, and rock away!

BONE ALLEY

Head bone ache and the neck bone snap
Collarbone creak and the rib bone crack
Backbone break and the hipbone sore
Don't want to shake like it shook no more
Oh . . . rolling along

Thigh bone, knee bone, leg bone, shin
You can't walk out and you don't walk in
Ankle bone twist and the foot bone flat
Got to keep rolling in spite of that
Oh, rolling along

I know you know I know too
but I can't tell you who else knew
Fit my bones like a rattlesnake skin
You opened the window and I crawled in
Oh . . . rolling along

Hipbone, thigh bone, knee bone, shin
Ankle bone, elbow, who walks in?
Your mother, your father, the man with the lease
the feds and the Northwest Mounted Police
Oh . . . rolling along

Thigh bone, knee bone, leg bone, shin
It's your party so walk on in
Don't get worried who's doing what to
Keep on rollin' like you're s'posed to do
Oh . . . rolling along

Head bone, neck bone, collarbone alley
Rib bone, backbone, hipbone alley
Thigh bone, knee bone, leg bone alley
Shin bone, ankle bone, foot bone alley
Oh . . . rolling along

BOOK OF DANIEL

Calling down the gods of gold, silver, stone, and wood
The mighty king of Babylon, the proud Belshazzar, stood
Drinking glory to himself as though he were a god
When an armless hand appeared among that party crowd
Came drifting through the window to write upon the wall
Four words that didn't make much sense at all

The king turned to his friends in fright, in frenzied desperation
But not one soul among them could make interpretation
The queen said: Long ago there was a wise man in this land;
Why don't you send for Daniel? He could read them

Daniel walked in bent but tall, spat upon the floor
Let me see these words . . . well, hmm—yes . . . I've seen them before
They simply mean your days are numbered; fact, they're even run
You've been judged in the balance and found wanting
Your royalty is just a gift—your father learned that lesson
By losing both his kingdom and his reason

So great in pride he was cut down, driven to the field—
Lived there like a wild beast until his pride did yield
And when the king, your father, achieved humility
He was restored his kingdom and his sanity

And though you knew all this to start you humbled not your heart
The writing on the wall commands your fall!
Old King Darius that night slew Belshazzar
Appointed Daniel prince and first adviser
The lesser princes being jealous, drew up a decree
Allowing prayer to no one but the king

They caught old Daniel dead to rights down upon his knees
Threw him in the lion's den for breaking that decree
Daniel walked among them safely, by his faith protected
The king said: This is just what I expected
Now you who brought me Daniel may kindly go yourselves
Into the lion's den—see how you fare there

What shall be the end of this? How shall it pass away?
Get up, old Daniel, never mind, get up and go thy way
Further words are closed and sealed until the end of time
Many shall be called, each in his season
In wickedness of pride is lost the light to understand
How little grace is earned and how much given

BORN SIDESTEPPER

Pumpkin on a sweet tater vine
That's a sure sign
you're gonna be rich
You may have to pay
but you do that anyway
Anyway . . .

Born with one foot out the door
You're a born sidestepper
You try to deny
but you can't sidestep it
You know you're in love once more
Once more . . .

Storm cloud but it won't last the day
Feeling so lost
You know what it cost
It cost all you got
and you still can't believe you've paid
You've paid . . .

Years die but love do not weep
New ones coming along
They're bound to go wrong
Cost you your sleep
but they don't have to cut too deep
Not forever . . .

Born on the crest of a wind
You go where it blows
The highs and the lows
You're a born sidestepper
But you know you're in love again

You can't sidestep it
You know you're in love
No, you can't sidestep it
You know you're in love again

(Woke up one morning and wrote this down straight out of a dream—or as straight as these things can be—where it was accompanied by a haunting melody that I've never been able to duplicate)

25

BOX OF RAIN

Look out of any window
any morning, any evening, any day
Maybe the sun is shining
birds are winging or
rain is falling from a heavy sky—
What do you want me to do,
to do for you to see you through?
For this is all a dream we dreamed
one afternoon long ago

Walk out of any doorway
feel your way, feel your way
like the day before
Maybe you'll find direction
around some corner
where it's been waiting to meet you—
What do you want me to do,
to watch for you while you're sleeping?
Well, please don't be surprised
when you find me dreaming, too

Look into any eyes
you find by you, you can see
clear through to another day
I know it's been seen before
through other eyes on other days
while going home—
What do you want me to do,
to do for you to see you through?
It's all a dream we dreamed
one afternoon long ago

Walk into splintered sunlight
Inch your way through dead dreams
to another land
Maybe you're tired and broken
Your tongue is twisted
with words half spoken
and thoughts unclear
What do you want me to do
to do for you to see you through?
A box of rain will ease the pain
and love will see you through

It's just a box of rain
I don't know who put it there
Believe it if you need it
or leave it if you dare
But it's just a box of rain
or a ribbon for your hair
Such a long, long time to be gone
and a short time to be there

(Phil Lesh wanted a song to sing to his dying father and had composed a piece complete with every vocal
nuance but the words. If ever a lyric "wrote itself," this did—as fast as the pen would pull.)

BOYS IN THE BARROOM

Does God look down on the boys in the barroom,
Mainly forsaken but surely not judged?
Jacks, kings, and aces, their faces in wine—
Do Lord deliver our kind

From singing for whiskey
Three strings on the fiddle
Four on the guitar
And a song that I love
Many's the night spent
Picking and singing
In hopes it be pleasing
Both here and above

Jack string fiddle to my sawtooth bow
Who loves loneliness loves it alone
I love the dim lights like some love the dew
Only thing I wonder sometimes—

Does God look down on the boys in the barroom
Mainly forsaken but surely not judged?
Jacks, kings, and aces, their faces in wine—
Do Lord deliver our kind

BROKE-DOWN PALACE

Fare you well, my honey
Fare you well, my only true one
All the birds that were singing
Have flown except you alone

Going to leave this broke-down palace
On my hands and my knees I will roll, roll, roll
Make myself a bed by the waterside
In my time—in my time—I will roll, roll, roll

In a bed, in a bed
by the waterside I will lay my head
Listen to the river sing sweet songs
to rock my soul

River gonna take me
Sing me sweet and sleepy
Sing me sweet and sleepy
all the way back home
It's a far-gone lullaby
sung many years ago
Mama, Mama, many worlds I've come
since I first left home

Going home, going home
by the waterside I will rest my bones
Listen to the river sing sweet songs
to rock my soul

Going to plant a weeping willow
On the bank's green edge, it will grow, grow, grow
Sing a lullaby beside the water
Lovers come and go—the river roll, roll, roll

Fare you well, fare you well
I love you more than words can tell
Listen to the river sing sweet songs
to rock my soul

BROWN-EYED WOMEN

Gone are the days when the ox fall down
he'd take up the yoke and plow the
      fields around
Gone are the days when the ladies said:
      "Please,
gently, Jack Jones, won't you come
      to me?"

Brown-eyed women and red grenadine
the bottle was dusty but the liquor
      was clean
Sound of the thunder with the rain
      pouring down
and it looks like the old man's getting on

In 1920 when he stepped to the bar
he drank to the dregs of the whiskey jar
In 1930 when the Wall caved in
he paid his way selling red-eye gin

Brown-eyed women and red grenadine
the bottle was dusty but the liquor
      was clean
Sound of the thunder with the rain
      pouring down
and it looks like the old man's getting on

Delilah Jones was the mother of twins
two times over and the rest was sins
Raised eight boys, only I turned bad
Didn't get the lickings that the other
      ones had

Brown-eyed women and red grenadine
the bottle was dusty but the liquor
      was clean
Sound of the thunder with the rain
      pouring down
and it looks like the old man's getting on

Tumbledown shack in Bigfoot County
Snowed so hard that the roof caved in
Delilah Jones went to meet her God
and the old man never was the same again

Brown-eyed women and red grenadine
the bottle was dusty but the liquor
      was clean
Sound of the thunder with the rain
      pouring down
and it looks like the old man's getting on

Daddy made whiskey and he made it well
Cost two dollars and it burned like hell
I cut hick'ry to fire the still
Drink down a bottle and you're ready
      to kill

Brown-eyed women and red grenadine
the bottle was dusty but the liquor
      was clean
Sound of the thunder with the rain
      pouring down
and it looks like the old man's getting on

BUILT TO LAST

There are times when you can beckon
There are times when you must call
You can take a lot of reckoning
But you can't take it all
There are times when I can help you out
And times that you must fall
There are times when you must live
    in doubt
And I can't help at all

Three blue stars/Rise on the hill
Say no more, now/Just be still
All these trials/Soon be past
Look for something/Built to last

A wind held by the collar
Got a cloud held by the breeze
You can walk on coals of fire
But sometimes you must freeze
There are times when you offend me
And I do the same to you
If we can't or won't forget it,
I guess we could be through

One blue star/Sets on the hill
Call it back/You never will
One more star/Sinks in the past
Show me something/Built to last.

Built to last till time itself
Falls tumbling from the wall
Built to last till sunshine fails
And darkness moves on all
Built to last while years roll past
Like cloudscapes in the sky
Show me something built to last
Or something built to try

There are times when you get hit upon
Try hard but you cannot give
Other times you'd gladly part
With what you need to live
Don't waste your breath to save your face
When you have done your best
And even more is asked of you
Fate will decide the rest.

All the stars/Are gone but one
Morning breaks/Here comes the sun
Cross the sky/Now sinking fast
Show me something/Built to last

Three blue stars/Rise on the hill
Say no more, now/Just be still
All these trials/Soon be past
Look for something/Built to last

One blue star/Sets on the hill
Call it back/You never will
One more star/Sinks in the past
Show me something/Built to last

All the stars/Are gone but one
Morning breaks/Here comes the sun
Cross the sky/Now sinking fast
Show me something/Built to last

CANDYMAN

Come all you pretty women
with your hair hanging down
Open up your windows 'cause
the Candyman's in town
Come on, boys, and gamble
Roll those laughing bones
Seven come eleven, boys
I'll take your money home

Look out
Look out
The Candyman
Here he come
and he's gone again
Pretty lady ain't
got no friend
till the Candyman
come 'round again

I come in from Memphis
where I learned to talk the jive
When I get back to Memphis
be one less man alive
Good mornin', Mr. Benson
I see you're doin' well
If I had me a shotgun
I'd blow you straight to Hell

Look out
Look out
The Candyman
Here he come
and he's gone again
Pretty lady ain't
got no friend

till the Candyman
come 'round again

Come on, boys, and wager
if you have got the mind
If you got a dollar, boys
lay it on the line
Hand me my old guitar
Pass the whiskey 'round
Want you to tell everybody you meet
the Candyman's in town

Look out
Look out
The Candyman
Here he come
and he's gone again
Pretty lady ain't
got no friend
till the Candyman
come 'round again

CASEY JONES

This old engine
makes it on time
Leaves Central Station
at a quarter to nine
Hits River Junction
at seventeen to
at a quarter to ten
you know it's trav'lin' again

Drivin' that train
High on Cocaine
Casey Jones, you better
watch your speed
Trouble ahead
Trouble behind
and you know that notion
just crossed my mind

Trouble ahead
The Lady in Red
Take my advice
you be better off dead
Switchman sleepin'
Train hundred and two
is on the wrong track and
headed for you

Drivin' that train
High on Cocaine
Casey Jones, you better
watch your speed
Trouble ahead
Trouble behind
and you know that notion
just crossed my mind

Trouble with you is
The trouble with me
Got two good eyes
but we still don't see
Come 'round the bend
You know it's the end
The fireman screams and
The engine just gleams

Drivin' that train
High on Cocaine
Casey Jones, you better
watch your speed
Trouble ahead
Trouble behind
and you know that notion
just crossed my mind

CATS UNDER THE STARS

Cats on the blacktop
Birdy in the treetop
Someone plays guitar that
sounds like clavinette
I ain't ready yet
to go to bed
Think I'll take a walk
downtown instead

Cats on the bandstand
Give 'em each a big hand
Anyone who sweats that hard
must be all right
No one wants a fight
No black eye
Just another cat beneath
the stars tonight

Cats in the limelight
Feels like it's all right
Everybody wants something
they may not get
I ain't ready yet
It ain't complete
That's why I'm heading down
to Alley Cat Street

A satin blouse unbuttoning
Time's a stripper
Doing it just for you

Knock in the brass tacks
Cover up your tracks, Jack
You ain't nowhere till
you can pay your own way back
What else do you lack
to make it right
but cats down under
the stars tonight?

(The Garcia Band was scheduled to take a month-long break from recording the 1978 album named after this song so Ron Tutt could do his day job: drumming for the Elvis tour. Within a week recording was able to resume due to unforeseen circumstances.)

CHILDREN'S LAMENT

When a child is being born
Cut the cord and tie a knot
Be sure you cut it with a keen blade
Life is short and full of thorns

Clear his throat
Be sure he cries out
Wash him clean and keep him warm
You gave him life
The truest thing you'll ever give
And his time will come
When your work is done
When your work is done

Won't you sing, Melinda
Won't you sing for me?
While the rain
While the rain is falling down
Slowly falls the rain outside
Won't you sing, Melinda, sing
Won't you sing
One last song for me?

In the hour of your dying
Point your breath and think away
In one brief moment
All eternity comes clear

Give yourself unto the light
Gladly
Have no fear
It gave you life
The only thing it has to give
And your time will come
When your work is done
When your work is done

Won't you sing, Melinda
Won't you sing for me?
While the rain
While the rain is falling down
Slowly falls the rain outside
Won't you sing, Melinda, sing
Won't you sing
One last song for me?

CHINA CAT SUNFLOWER

Look for a while at the China Cat Sunflower
proud-walking jingle in the midnight sun
Copper-dome bodhi drip a silver kimono
like a crazy-quilt star gown
through a dream night wind

Krazy Kat peeking through a lace bandana
like a one-eyed Cheshire
like a diamond-eye Jack
A leaf of all colors plays
a golden string fiddle
to a double-*e* waterfall over my back

Comic book colors on a violin river
crying Leonardo words
from out a silk trombone
I rang a silent bell
beneath a shower of pearls
in the eagle wing palace
of the Queen Chinee

(Nobody ever asked me the meaning of this song. People seem to know exactly what I'm talking about.
It's good that a few things in this world are clear to all of us.)

CHINA DOLL

A pistol shot at five o'clock
The bells of heaven ring
Tell me what you done it for
"No, I won't tell you a thing

"Yesterday I begged you
before I hit the ground—
all I leave behind me
is only what I found

"If you can abide it
let the hurdy-gurdy play—
Stranger ones have come by here
before they flew away

"I will not condemn you
nor yet would I deny . . ."
I would ask the same of you
but failing will not die. . . .

Take up your china doll
it's only fractured—
and just a little nervous
from the fall

CHINGO!

Long come a Witchman chew on an onion
Sing to a spider sat on this thumb
Great big stars like blood–red diamonds
Brew in the bucket—now give me one

Baia bell-a-ringo
Chingo!
Look out, Monkeyman
Buck and run
Horse and rider
Pale blue lightning
Rose-red thunder
You're the one

I'm in love with the Witchman's daughter
Aggravates my soul to say
Once in the cane I nearly caught her
She turned to a bird and flew away

Baia bell-a-ringo
Chingo!
Dark of the morning
Bright blue sun
Look out, Monkeyman
Here come Shango
Knife and bow
And whip and gun

Been too long on Dead Man's Hill
Feet won't move but I can't lay still
Monkeyman, I come for your daughter
Give her up of your free goodwill

Baia bell-a-ringo
Chingo!

Look out, Monkeyman
Buck and run
Horse and rider
Pale blue lightning
Tell your daughter
Her time has come!

Baia bell-a-ringo
Chingo! Chingo!
Baia bell-a-ringo
All night long
Baia bell-a-ringo
Chingo! Chingo!
Look out, Monkeyman
I'm your son
Baia bell-a-ringo
Chingo! Chingo!
Baia bell-a-ringo
All night long

CIRCULATE THE RHYTHM

Circulate the rhythm in action
Ride it till it's out of fashion
Who'll pay rent? I don't know
Spent all mine on a rock-and-roll show
One more rider at the end of the trail hoping
Miracles happen when everything else fails

Circulate the rhythm in action
Dig on in and don't lose traction
Call it what you want, I don't care
Whatever it takes to get it there
Honey, if it makes you feel all right
Leave it at the top of the hill tonight

Fill my days with circulating rhythm
Where they spill I will spill with them
Dip my bucket in the running stream
Try to go with it whatever that means

Circulate, circulate the rhythm
Circulate the rhythm right now
Circulate the rhythm right
Circulate, circulate
Circulate the rhythm right now

Circulate the rhythm wherever it leads to
Lose no sleep over how they treat you
Lovers go but love remains
Everything else goes up in flames
Hearts were made to break in two
Till nothing at all but the beat shines through

Fill my heart with circulating rhythm
Days go by and I go with them
Who'll pay rent?—Honey, I don't know
Knock on the door and glass in the window

Circulate, circulate the rhythm
Circulate the rhythm right now
Circulate the rhythm right
Circulate, circulate
Circulate the rhythm right now

Sail away, pack of dreams
You were never what you seem
Hold on, hold tight
Circulate the rhythm right
Circulate the rhythm in action
Ride it in and out of fashion
Count your change at the end of the trail
Miracles happen when everything else fails

COME AND GET IT

Solomon and Samson/Moving into town
One of 'em to build it up/and one to tear it down
Get a move on/Baby, I believe it's time to leave this town
Right or wrong/Movin' on

What I want I haven't got and what I got I need
I can take a kick or two but I don't want to bleed
Come and get it/Get it while the getting is really good
If you think you could/Stand on the rock where Moses stood

Kamikaze Cadillac, I can't afford the pace
Got an application in to join the human race
Get a move on/Honey, I believe it's time to leave this town
Right or wrong/Come and get it, let's move it on

Going where a dollar buys a dollar worth of change
Rolling down the lonesome road/feeling mighty strange
Come and get it/Get it while the getting is to be got
Come and get it/Later decide if you need it or not

Lay it down in detail/Savage, cool, and sweet
Just how low and lonesome did you get on Lonely Street?
Get a move on/I'm dead-ready to blow this town
Right or wrong/Movin' on

Help yourself to seconds but go easy on the cake till you get
yourself a stomach for the supper that you make
Come and get it/Get it while the getting is to be had
Once you got it/If you don't like it, that's too damn bad

Laminated backstage universal pass
To a junkyard wonderland through the looking glass
Get a move on/I believe it's time to leave this town
Right or wrong/Movin' on

Some dogs got an hour/Others got a day
I got seven minutes/Five have slipped away
Come and get it/Get it while the getting is extra great
Come and get it/Hungry or not, get down and lick that plate

Come and get it/Any fish is fine if you got good bait
Hesitation Blues/Tell me, how long do I have to wait?
Comes the dawn/Beg your pardon, I'm movin' on

Come and get it/They're laughing on cue behind the green door
Come and get it/Question of mind over metaphor
Come and get it/Mose kicked the bucket; fact, he bought the store
Come and get it/Ain't gonna grieve his lord no more
Come and get it/Are you here after what I'm here for?
Come and get it/Jukin' in the channel till my chaps are sore
Come and get it/Hang your head and cry from four till late
Come and get it/I hope you can shimmy like your sister Kate
Come and get it/Might like to try it on at any rate
Come and get it/Ooo, shimmy like your sister Kate

COMES A TIME

Comes a time
when the blind man
takes your hand
says: Don't you see?
got to make it somehow
on the dreams you still believe
Don't give it up
you've got an empty cup
only love can fill
only love can fill

Been walking all morning
Went walking all night
I can't see much difference
between the dark and the light
And I feel the wind
And I taste the rain
Never in my mind
to cause so much pain

Comes a time
when the blind man
takes your hand
says: Don't you see?
got to make it somehow
on the dreams you still believe
Don't give it up
you've got an empty cup
only love can fill
only love can fill

From day to day
just letting it ride
you get so far away
from how it feels inside

You can't let go
'cause you're afraid to fall
till the day may come
when you can't feel at all

Comes a time
when the blind man
takes your hand
says: Don't you see?
got to make it somehow
on the things you still believe
Don't give it up
you've got an empty cup
only love can fill
only love can fill

COME TO LIFE

Everything
Everything has come to life again
No one doubted but the ice got thin
What came too soon was so hard to keep
So full a harvest it was hard to reap

There were days
Seemed just like the walls would crumble
Shoot from the hip and pray for trouble
Stone-cold sober and seeing double
How that midnight band could ramble
Taking mansions and leaving shambles

Remember other times and places
Last night's dance
the glowing faces
All the lights and shadows in the hall
Seeking higher peaks from which to fall

Remember we were telling you
that time would stop and nations fall
Now we find the lies come true
Can you tell me, tell me, tell me
What are we to do?

Because the good old days
Those good old days are all dead and gone
Good-bye and bless them all, every one
What was true has passed the test
Just as well forget the rest
Half of what you saw was not yours to know
Let it go

(This is the first of my lyrics ever to make it onto a number-one album: the Jefferson Starship's *Dragonfly*.)

COSMIC CHARLEY

Cosmic Charley, how do you do?
Truckin' in style along the avenue
Dumdeedumdee doodley doo
Go on home, your mama's calling you

Calico Kahlia, come tell me the news
Calamity's waiting for a way to get to her
Rosy red and electric blue
I bought you a paddle for your paper canoe

Say you'll come back when you can
Whenever your airplane happens to land
Maybe I'll be back here, too
It all depends on what's with you

Hung up waiting for a windy day
Kite on ice since the first of February
Mama Bee saying that the wind might blow
But standing here I say I just don't know

New ones comin as the old ones go
Everything's movin here but much too slowly
Little bit quicker and we might have time
to say "How do you do?" before we're left behind

Calliope wail like a seaside zoo
The very last lately inquired about you
It's really very one or two
The first you wanted, the last I knew

I just wonder if you shouldn't feel
less concern about the deep unreal
The very first word is: How do you do?
The last: Go home, your mama's calling you

Go on home
Your mama's calling you
Calling you. . . .

CRAZY FINGERS

Your rain falls like crazy fingers
Peals of fragile thunder keeping time

Recall the days that still are to come
Some sing blue

Hang your heart on laughing willow
Stray down to the water
Deep Sea of Love

Beneath the sweet calm face of the sea
Swift undertow

Life may be sweeter for this, I don't know
See how it feels in the end
May Lady Lullaby sing plainly for you
Soft, strong, sweet and true

Cloud hands reaching from a rainbow
Tapping at the window touch your hair

So swift and bright
Strange figures of light
Float in air

Who can stop what must arrive now?
Something new is waiting to be born

Dark as the night
You're still by my side
Shining side

Gone are the days we stopped to decide
Where we should go
We just ride

Gone are the broken eyes we saw through
     in dreams
Gone—both dream and lie

Life may be sweeter for this I don't know
Feels like it might be alright
While Lady Lullaby sings plainly for you
Love still rings true

Midnight on a carousel ride
Reaching for the gold ring down inside

Never could reach
It just slips away but I try

("Crazy Fingers" is a collection of haiku-style verses, mostly seventeen syllables, some more successful than others, with no connecting link other than similarity of mood.)

CROOKED JUDGE

Paid my money to a crooked judge
Set out to find an honest man
That's how I came to be in Boston
looking like I am

If by now we stop to sleep
we can't make no midnight creep
Only time can ever say
Pack my cat and haul away

Rained all night and it rained all day
Rain come floated my house away
Didn't it rain oh didn't it rain?
Didn't it rain that day!

If by now we step by, then
someday we may meet again
Run down high, look down low
Call the Captain up from the hole

I was down in some low dive
talkin all the usual jive
like: Say Buddy gimme five
I ain't drunk enough to drive

Wipe that grin right off your face
before I throw you through the wall
No one needs a wise guy, Jack
Specially one don't check his facts

If by now we step by, then
someday we may meet again

Who cares what you have to say?
Even this too shall pass away
Even this too shall pass away
Hey, hey, crooked judge
even this too shall pass away

(David Nelson said he once had a dream about ordering up lyrics from me like hamburgers from a fry cook.
Here's one for the New Riders with relish but no mayo.)

CRUEL WHITE WATER

Up near the border where the cruel white water
drowns the vagabond that sleeps too low
me and my companion, the famous Jack O'Lanterns
tracked the misty mountain through the snow

Ran across the hidden chord, couldn't learn the changes
The blue Pacific called, I had to go
There was holly on the ivy in the apparition mountains
but the warmest bed I found was ten below

Courted Lady Greensleeves, she threw me out the window
I landed like a feather in the trees
Took off across New Mexico and landed in the Bayou
The catfish was too lean, I had to blow

Don't lie for gold, no-no-no-no
Don't lie for love, that turns out cold
If life depends, just get out whole
Don't lie for less, no-no-no-no

Marie, Marie—Marie Helena
You're my amour, you're my own heart
Marie—Marie Helena
Marie, Marie—Marie Helene

Left the life of ease and caught the black iron steamer
cross the barren waste to your arcade
I sang take me to your leader in my strangest country tenor
but the bed I meant to lay was halfway made

Left overpieces aren't exactly what I needed
They didn't have much meaning on their own
Was some talk of deviation, from what was never mentioned
So I set out to find the wrong way home

Home inside the hour, tuning my guitar
I get this sudden urge I know so well
I finished my rendition of *don't pity my condition*
then looked around to find what I could sell

Can't sell your soul, leave that alone
Can't change your role, Big Daddy Low
Don't break your back for less than love
Don't trade your love for stars above
No no no Marie—Marie Helena
You're my amour, you're my own heart
Marie—Marie Helena
Marie, Marie—Marie Helene

Caught up with Jack O'Lanterns in a town called Make It Hurt
preaching three-card monte in the Live and Let It Church
The choir was down and dirty, drawin' bad and bettin' worse
We left at ten to six in a padded hearse

I might find companions in the after-hour taverns
To tell a tale or two I never heard
but the strangest song I know
is what the thunder says to lightning
and I never could recall a single word
. . . except . . .
Up near the border where the cruel white water
drowns the vagabond that sleeps too low
me and my companion, the famous Jack O'Lanterns
tracked the misty mountain through the snow

Don't lie for gold, no-no-no-no
Don't lie for love, that turns out cold
If life depends, just get out whole
Don't lie for less, no-no-no-no
Marie, Marie—Marie Helena
by firelight—you steal my heart
Oh Marie—Marie Helena
Marie, Marie—Marie Helena

CRY DOWN THE YEARS

Sing a song of shadows shifting in a shadow play
Forgot to wind the sundial, now it's stuck on yesterday
Other side of paradise the lamplight of the lost
Shines from distant summer, Love, but who can count the cost?

Cry down the centuries
Cry down the years
Cry down the ages
Cry down the years

Sing a song of human hope to shadows in the dust
In places where the sun rises only 'cause it must
Where the cold machinery in which we dare to trust
grinds the grain for seven loaves, delivers up a crust

Cry down the centuries
Cry down the years
Cry down the ages
Cry down the years

Spyrogyra twist inside a microscopic drop
Every now and then another rises to the top
Tells you, "I've seen everything—of that which might be seen
But I can't call the shots for you/I don't know what it means"

Cry down the centuries
Cry down the years
Cry down the ages
Cry down the years

When I say I love you, don't decide to take it wrong
Or else come on blasé as though you knew it all along
If on a winter's night a traveler happens by your door
Listen to his fairy tale but do not ask for more

Cry down the centuries
Cry down the years
Cry down the ages
Cry down the years

Wrap your dreams around you like a cloak against the cold
Never share them carelessly or force them to unfold
None so lonely as the brave when conscience overrules
The wisdom of hypocrisy; the common sense of fools

Cry down the centuries
Cry down the years
Cry down the ages
Cry down the years

CRY IN THE NIGHT

What was that cry I heard in the night?
That was no cry, child, that was the wind
What was that crash, what fell to the floor?
Just the branch of a tree or the slam of a door

Who was that man I saw running away?
That was no man, that was just Thomas Gray
What did he hold in his hand like a knife?
Only a candle he brought to his wife

Then it must be a candle to light her to Hell
Hush you, child, you must never tell
Those were just dreams you had in the night
Now pack up quickly, we must leave before light

If we leave before day we can run by the moon
Hurry, we cannot get started too soon
When you grow older and think like a man
Some of these things you may understand

Ring on the bell it was twenty years past
Each year I think I knew less the last
But I'm sure as I'm certain my name is not Gray
The roots of this matter shall not pass away

Who's in this drawing that looks just like me
I found in your Bible, say, who can it be?
That's just a servant we called Thomas White
Who was hanged from the gate post by dawn's early light

Who gave you this ring I found in your sack?
A very nice boy whom we called Thomas Black
I'll tell you no more, you just think through the night
No doubt the conclusions you draw will be right

There's more threads that bind us than you'll ever know
More chains inside us than chains that we show
The past that divides is now better forgot
Lest thoughts of revenge twist those threads in a knot

CUMBERLAND BLUES

I can't stay much longer, Melinda
The sun is getting high
I can't help you with your troubles
If you won't help with mine

I gotta get down
I gotta get down
Got to get down to the mine

You keep me up just one more night
I can't sleep here no more
Little Ben clock says quarter to eight
You kept me up till four

I gotta get down
I gotta get down
Or I can't work there no more

Lotta poor man make a five-dollar bill
Keep him happy all the time
Some other fellow making nothing at all
And you can hear him cryin' . . .

"Can I go, buddy
Can I go down
Take your shift at the mine?"

Got to get down to the Cumberland Mine
That's where I mainly spend my time
Make good money/five dollars a day
Made any more I might move away—

Lotta poor man got the Cumberland Blues
He can't win for losin'
Lotta poor man got to walk the line
Just to pay his union dues

I don't know now
I just don't know
If I'm goin' back again
I don't know now
I just don't know
If I'm goin' back again

(The best compliment I ever had on a lyric was from an old guy who'd worked at the Cumberland mine. He said: "I wonder what the guy who wrote this song would've thought if he'd ever known something like the Grateful Dead was gonna do it.")

DANCE A HOLE

Protected dreams of jealousy
leave nothing worth forsaking
Judge the matter how you will
that prize is not worth taking

Dance a hole right through the floorboard
Dance a hole right through your shoe
When the midnight show is over
what else have you got to do?

Roll away the half-blind vision
dressed in stars by winter light
Close the door to crippled highways
song by song that filled the night
Bend it into unclear spaces
Save the eye but lose the sight
Does it matter when it's over
if the truth was even right?

You can play with power and money
You can play with towers above
Draw the line there, if you're able
Don't you ever play with love
Don't play with love
Don't you ever play with love

A hundred pipers on the highway
Blink your eye, they're gone again
Crimson stars on blue-white banners
westward ho! through ten years' rain
Outraged senses cry: *Be numb,*
you just cause us further pain
Still the neon river beckons
Star-crossed lovers bloom again

Dance a hole right through the floorboard
Dance a hole right through your shoe
In the hour 'tween blood and roses
what else have you got to do?

Could you break the gray, cold vision,
come to terms with what you can?
Proceed from there, if you're able
with just the ground on which you stand?
The past is not the only highway
Why go roll it out again?
The future's in the unborn river
of this morning's cloudless rain

In my lady's winter palace
dreamward as the summer lies
I mistook a flight of swallows
for the questions in your eyes

Broken words defending highways
Shining bright like April rain
Loving lies and wrong decisions
Yes, I guess it comes again
Yes, I guess it comes again

Dance a hole right through the floorboard
Dance a hole right through your shoe
In the hour 'tween blood and roses
what else have you got to do?

DARK STAR

Dark star crashes
pouring its light
into ashes

Reason tatters
the forces tear loose
from the axis

Searchlight casting
for faults in the
clouds of delusion

Shall we go,
you and I
while we can?
Through
the transitive nightfall
of diamonds

Mirror shatters
in formless reflections
of matter

Glass hand dissolving
to ice-petal flowers
revolving

Lady in velvet
recedes
in the nights of good-bye

Shall we go,
you and I
while we can?
Through
the transitive nightfall
of diamonds

spinning a set the stars through which the tattered tales
    of axis roll
about the waxen wind of never set to motion in the
    unbecoming
round about the reason hardly matters nor the wise
    through which
the stars were set in spin

(Though they arranged "Alligator," "China Cat Sunflower," and "Saint Stephen" to lyrics I mailed Garcia from New Mexico, this is the first lyric I wrote *with* the Grateful Dead.)

54

DEAL

Since it cost a lot to win
and even more to lose
You and me bound to spend some time
wondering what to choose

Goes to show you don't ever know
Watch each card you play
and play it slow
Wait until your deal come round
Don't you let that deal go down

I been gambling hereabouts
for ten good solid years
If I told you all that went down
it would burn off both your ears

It goes to show you don't ever know
Watch each card you play
and play it slow
Wait until your deal come round
Don't you let that deal go down

Since you poured the wine for me
and tightend up my shoes
I hate to leave you sitting there
composin' lonesome blues

It goes to show you don't ever know
Watch each card you play
and play it slow
Wait until your deal come round
Don't you let that deal go down
Don't you let that deal go down, no
Don't you let your deal go down

DELIA DELYON AND STAGGERLEE

1940 Xmas evening with a full moon over town
Staggerlee met Bill DeLyon
and he blew that poor boy down
Do you know what he shot him for?
What do you make of that?
'Cause Billy DeLyon threw lucky dice,
won Staggerlee's Stetson hat

Baio, Baio, tell me how can this be?
You arrest the girls for turning tricks
but you're scared of Staggerlee
Staggerlee is a madman and he shot my Billy dead
Baio you go get him or give the job to me

Delia DeLyon, dear sweet Delia-D
How the hell can I arrest him when he's twice as big as me?
Don't ask me to go downtown—I wouldn't come back alive
Not only is that mother *big* but he packs a .45

Baio Delia said *just give me a gun*
He shot my Billy dead now I'm gonna see him hung
She waded to DeLyon's Club through Billy DeLyon's blood
Stepped up to Staggerlee at the bar
Said *Buy me a gin fizz, love*

As Staggerlee lit a cigarette she shot him in the balls
Blew the smoke off her revolver, had him dragged to city hall
Baio, Baio, see you hang him high
He shot my Billy dead and now he's got to die

Delia went a-walking down on Singapore Street
A three-piece band on the corner played "Nearer My God to Thee"
but Delia whistled a different tune . . . what tune could it be?

The song that woman sung was *Look out Staggerlee*
The song that Delia sung was *Look out Staggerlee*
The song that woman sung was *Look out Staggerlee*
The song that Delia sung was *Look out Staggerlee*

DINOSAUR

It's strictly a temporary gig
It's a Dinosaur and I hope you dig
it's born from a sense of discontent
at a good beginning somehow bent
And I know—yes, I know
it's going nowhere
it's already there
discovered that there's nowhere to go

It's strictly a temporary scene
It's a Dinosaur, do you know what I mean?
Born in the jungle at the dawn of time
singing: *Baby, baby, don't lose your mind*
'Cause I know—yes, I know
it's all dressed up with nowhere to go
but it loves you
and it tells you so

It's strictly a temporary groove
Got a lot of love and not a lot to prove
It's got shoo-doot'n dooby-dooby-doo
It looks like me and it sounds like you
And I know—well, I know
that growing old with rock and roll
is the best a poor boy can do

D-I-N-O-S-A-U-R
What you see is what you are
Twinkle, twinkle little star
D-I-N-O-S-A-U-R
Living out these long, cold days
Sole survivor in a frozen waste
D-I-N-O-S-A-U-R
A dinosaur is what you are. . . .

(I joined the Dinosaurs [Barry Melton, Spencer Dryden, Peter Albin, and John Cippolino] in the mid-1980s, and this was intended as an anthem for the group.)

DIRE WOLF

In the timbers of Fennario
the wolves are running 'round
The winter was so hard and cold
froze ten feet 'neath the ground

Don't murder me
I beg of you, don't murder me
Please
don't murder me

I sat down to my supper
'Twas a bottle of red whiskey
I said my prayers and went to bed
That's the last they saw of me

Don't murder me
I beg of you, don't murder me
Please
don't murder me

When I awoke the Dire Wolf
Six hundred pounds of sin
Was grinning at my window
All I said was "Come on in"

Don't murder me
I beg of you, don't murder me
Please
don't murder me

The wolf came in, I got my cards
We sat down for a game
I cut my deck to the Queen of Spades
but the cards were all the same

Don't murder me
I beg of you, don't murder me
Please
don't murder me

In the backwash of Fennario
The black and bloody mire
The Dire Wolf collects his due
while the boys sing round the fire

Don't murder me
I beg of you, don't murder me
Please
don't murder me
I beg of you
Please
don't murder me

DO DENY (LYING MAN)

Live but to deceive
Say so to the jury, friend
And thus they do believe
I was born one reckless morn
Ten thousand years ago
Shaved and shorn, duly sworn
As down the road I go

Lying man/lying man/I deny
        /I'm a lying man
Do deny/do deny/do deny
        /I'm a lying man

Your truth is more than half a lie
My tales are halfway true
I say what occurs to me
and I don't check with you
Fan the fire to cool the flame
That's all I meant to do
Just treat me as though the hand
Were on the other shoe

Lying man/lying man/I deny
        /I'm a lying man
Do deny/do deny/do deny
        /I'm a lying man

Make the matter short and sweet
Convict or let me go
Considering my pedigree
how could you treat me so?
I who ate with Kate the Great
On Chinese silver plate
Who shot the shit with Sherman burnin'
down the Georgia state?

Lying man/lying man/I deny
        /I'm a lying man
Do deny/do deny/do deny
        /I'm a lying man

Folks believe whatever they need
to make them feel secure
Don't cast doubt upon my word
unless you know for sure
The Queen of Diamonds was my girl
when she was known as Lil
I never understood that girl
and I think I never will

Lying man/lying man
        /I deny/I'm a lying man
Do deny/do deny/do deny
        /I'm a lying man

Only thing I ever learned
of which I have no doubt
The skin sides on the inner side
to keep the cold side out
While you curse and kick yourself
and make believe to pray
I will tell you stories of
the one that got away

Lying man/lying man/I deny
        /I'm a lying man
Do deny/do deny/do deny
        /I'm a lying man

Before you even say hello
Here's how we could agree
You do what pleases you
And I do what pleases me
May such friendship never end
Our cup be full and deep
May our voices always blend
in our own harmonies

Lying man/lying man/I deny
        /I'm a lying man
Do deny/do deny/do deny
        /I'm a lying man

DOIN' THAT RAG

Sitting in Mangrove Valley chasing light beams
Everything wanders from baby to Z
Baby, baby, pretty, young on Tuesday
Old like a rum drinking demon at tea★

Baby, baby, tell me what's the matter
Why, why tell me, what's your why now?
Tell me why will you never come home?
Tell me what's your reason if you got a good one

Everywhere I go
The people all know
Everyone's doin' that rag

Take my line, go fishing for a Tuesday
Maybe take my supper, eat it down by the sea
Gave my baby twenty, forty good reasons
Couldn't find any better ones in the morning at three

Rain gonna come but the rain gonna go, you know
Stepping off sharply from the rank and file
Awful cold and dark like a dungeon
Maybe get a little bit darker 'fore the day

Hipsters, tripsters,
real cool chicks, sir,
everyone's doin' that rag

You needn't gild the lily, offer jewels to the sunset
No one is watching or standing in your shoes
Wash your lonely feet in the river in the morning
Everything promised is delivered to you

Don't neglect to pick up what your share is
All the winter birds are winging home now
Hey, Love, go and look around you
Nothing out there you haven't seen before now

★Peter Grant heard this line as "Old like a nun drinking demon bad tea."

But you can wade in the water
and never get wet
if you keep on doin' that rag

One-eyed jacks and the deuces are wild
The aces are crawling up and down your sleeve
Come back here, Baby Louise,
and tell me the name
of the game that you play

Is it all fall down?
Is it all go under?
Is it all fall down, down, down
Is it all go under?

Everywhere I go
the people all know
everybody's doin' that rag

DRUNKARD'S CAROL

Another cup for Heaven's sake
Before our way to slumber make
If one of us should fail to wake
His drunken soul may Jesus take

Two by two the tigers leap
While each to his own council keeps
Sail from shore to dreamless sleep
Upon the tears the angels weep

We were born for better things
Each and every man a king
If you will or not, we sing
Cause our voices loud to ring

Who is like our merry crowd?
They are damned few and we should be proud
If one of us should fail to wake
His drunken soul may Jesus take

DRY DUSTY ROAD

Dry dusty road
Dry dusty road
Brother, won't you carry me along
this dry dusty road?

Children shallying
Playing in the morning sun
Spike-heeled lady
running through the burying ground

You set my soul on fire
You set me on my own
Broke-down car but the wheels still roll
down the dry, dry dusty road

Stuck inside a tunnel
Beset with diamond lies
Wings of night enclosing
like a long, long night without a dawning

Being bent on ruin
I tried to sell my name
All that I got for it
was one good look at flame

Drive, drive, dusty road
Dry dusty road
Oh, brother, let me carry you along
this dry dusty road

In that flame I saw a face
I've never seen before
If they ask me why, I know
just who I done this for

No one else to come to
Not much else I know
Not much else I'm good for
Lay away my lady-o

You set my soul on fire
You set me on my own
Broke-down car but the wheels still roll
down the dry, dry dusty road

Dusty road, dry, dry dusty road
Dusty road . . . dry, dry . . . dusty road

DUPREE'S DIAMOND BLUES

When I was just a little young boy,
Papa said, "Son, you'll never get far,
I'll tell you the reason if you want to know,
'cause, child of mine, there isn't really very far to go"

Well, baby, baby wants a gold diamond ring
Wants it more than most any old thing
Well, when I get those jelly-roll blues
Why, I'd go and get anything in this world for you

Down to the jewelry store packing a gun,
says, "Wrap it up. I think I'll take this one."
"A thousand dollars, please," the jewelry man said
Dupree, he said, "I'll pay this one off to you in lead"

Well, you know, son, you just can't figure,
first thing you know you're gonna pull that trigger
and it's no wonder your reason goes bad—
jelly roll will drive you stone-mad

Judge said, "Son, this gonna cost you some time"
Dupree said, "Judge, you know that crossed my mind"
Judge said, "Fact, it's gonna cost you your life"
Dupree said, "Judge, you know that seems to me to be about right"

Well, baby, baby's gonna lose her sweet man
Dupree come out with a losing hand
Baby's gonna weep it up for a while
then go on out
and find another sweet man's gonna treat her with style

Judge said, "Son, I know your baby well
but that's a secret I can't never tell"
Dupree said, "Judge, well, it's well understood,
and you got to admit that that sweet, sweet jelly's so good"

Well, you know, son, you just can't figure,
first thing you know you're gonna pull that trigger
and it's no wonder your reason goes bad,
jelly roll will drive you stone-mad

Same old story and I know it's been told,
some like jelly-jelly—some like gold
Many a man's done a terrible thing
just to get baby that shiny diamond ring

EASY WIND

I been ballin' a shiny black steel jackhammer
Been chippin' up rocks for the great highway
Live five years if I take my time
Ballin' that jack and a drinkin' my wine

I been chippin' them rocks from dawn till doom
While my rider hide my bottle in the other room
Doctor say I better stop ballin' that jack
If I live five years gonna bust my back, yes I will

Easy wind cross the bayou today
There's a whole lotta women, mama,
Out in red on the streets today
And the river keep a talkin'
But you never hear a word it say

Gotta find a woman be good to me
Won't hide my liquor, try to serve me tea
'Cause I'm a stone jack baller and my heart is true
And I'll give everything that I got to you, yes I will

Easy wind blowing cross the bayou today
There's a whole lotta women, mama,
Out in red on the streets today
And the river keep a talkin'
But you never hear a word it say

EBOAY

Mighta been a rich man's son
If my father was not poor
Been living in the low coun-try
But I don't live there no more

Ee-bo-ay . . .
Yo mana mana
Some day soon
You will be cryin
Come to me
shim shim chamois
Lay away
You may be cryin
wo/oah—for
A long lost lover
Ay/Ay—or
A brand new rider
Eboay
Love is your master
Either way
Yo mana mana
Eboay
Yo mana mana
Eboay . . .

You work half your life to find
Some way to get inside
Wonder why you tell the truth
When it serves as well to lie

Ee-bo-ay/Yo mana mana /Some day soon—etc.

You might be a hell of a lover
We could all take a lesson from you
You could tell us how the stars all shine
And why the sky is blue

Ee-bo-ay/Yo mana mana /Some day soon—etc.

You work half your life to find
Some way to get back out
Others may say you've lost your mind
But you know what that's about

Ee-bo-ay/Yo mana mana /Some day soon—
etc.

Ee-bo-ay . . .
Yo mana mana
Some day soon
You will be cryin
Come to me
shim shim chamois
Lay away
You may be cryin
wo/oah—for
A long lost lover
Ay/Ay—or
A brand new rider
Eboay
Love is your master
Either way
Yo mana mana
Eboay
Yo mana mana
Eboay . . .

67

EIGHT BELOW ZERO

Eight below zero—too cold to snow
Eight below zero—nowhere to go
Oaks and the elms around Washington Square
Stark and contorted, twisted and bare
Shadows of twilight—lowering quick
Sullen as madness—brooding and thick
Bitter chill tears turn to ice if you cry
This is the city where dreams come to die

Fifth and MacDougall—crossing the street
The last rose of summer I happened to meet
She greeted my face with the back of her hand
I checked it for blood but made no reprimand.
"Been a long time," I said nonchalantly
She said "June 21st nineteen seventy three"
in a voice with inflections I've heard in my dreams
Where a long time ago's not so long as it seems

Eight below zero—too cold to snow
Eight below zero—nowhere to go
Eight below zero—face to the wind
Must of been written I'd meet you again

"I'll buy you some coffee," I said, "come inside;
Tell me who's living and tell me who's died.
Whatever happened to what-was-his-name?"
"Like all of the rest, he went back where he came."
I asked how it happened that she still remained
She laughed without humor: "I'd ask you the same.
You climbed up the ladder and stepped off the top.
You never were someone who knew when to stop."

"I'll stop when I'm buried," I said in reply
And ordered two pieces of blueberry pie.
She picked out the berries, neglected the crust,

"Like you," she said, "I never knew who to trust;
We never knew when and we never knew how.
We never got cheated, but look at us now.
You got protection—your gamble payed off—
But the fact you come back shows it wasn't enough."

Eight below zero—too cold to snow . . .

"You're talking in riddles," I said out of spite—
But deep in my heart—I could see she was right;
"I saw your last picture," she said "it was good . . .
It isn't my fault no one else understood."
She rolled up the crust in a tight little ball
Missed me by inches—it stuck on the wall.
She said "Leave me alone and go do what you do—
I got problems enough of my own without you.

"It's eight below zero and too cold to snow . . ."
Catching her drift, I made motions to go but
She stuck out her foot—my balance collapsed
I fell to my knees with my head in her lap.
I made up my mind to leave it right there,
Rightly or wrongly, I didn't much care
Familiar perfume from the lap of her dress . . .
Kingdoms have fallen defending much less.

Eight below zero—too cold to snow
Eight below zero—nowhere to go
Eight below zero—face to the wind
Must of been written I'd meet you again

THE ELEVEN

No more time to tell how
This is the season of what
Now is the time of returning
With thought jewels polished and gleaming

Now is the time past believing
The child has relinquished the reign
Now is the test of the boomerang
Tossed in the night of redeeming

Eight-sided whispering hallelujah hatrack
Seven-faced marble eye transitory dream doll
Six proud walkers on jingle-bell rainbow
Five men writing in fingers of gold
Four men tracking the great white sperm whale
Three girls wait in a foreign dominion
Ride in the whale belly
Fade away in moonlight
Sink beneath the waters
to the coral sand below
Now is the time of returning

ELIJAH

I sent you ribbons and I sent you rubies
And I sent you gold from the Bengal Bay
Sent a man to run and deliver
And another to fetch and carry for you

I sent silver buckets to carry your water
I set you a bucket of blood from the slaughter
I sent to know your turn of mind
Does it turn away or come around to me?

I find no pleasure, she said
So I want no pleasure
Go make my bed
Fill my pitcher with water
My pillow with straw
Elijah's gone and
I'd soon as not be dead

Still I thank thee, Lord
For the wonderful things
Full measure of which
No man can see
For the soup and the saddle
The boots and the bridle
And the Devil's own company

END OF THE ROAD

The highway wrapped around me like a python in the night
The moon howled at the ocean like some spirit lost in flight
Bruised and battered stars denounced the gallows of the sky
Like a pack of bandit angels strung up helplessly to die

My head was full of nothing but the pounding of the surf
And whirling kind of slowly like the spinning of the earth
Everything I lived for seemed played out like a joke
The all-night revelations and the poetry we spoke

This is the end of the road
Got no further passions to unload
Nothing left to do except explode
Here at the end of the road

Hitched a ride upon a cloud of sky-blue silver tin
Driven by an angel who had never tasted sin
God knows for one time in my life, I acted with reserve
When she asked Where I was going I said "Wherever I deserve"

She turned on the radio to 1948
Where Charlie Parker preached upon the saxophone of fate
I told my whole life story—she didn't bat an eye
Or shed one single tear; just looked ahead and sighed

This is the end of the road
Got no further passions to unload
Nothing left to do except explode
Here at the end of the road

Drove deep into the desert till the moon and stars were gone
The radio said *adios* as she dropped me off at dawn
I pulled out my last cigarette, she lit it with her eyes
Then sped off toward Sonora without even a good-bye

The kisses of the sun were sweet, I didn't even blink
Just let it pour into my eyes like some exotic drink
Cutting through the sand I saw the railing of a track
Leading on into forever with no hope of turning back

This is the end of the road
Got no further passions to unload
Nothing left to do except explode
Here at the end of the road

I left the years behind along with fear of growing old
As the trestles of the track turned to diamonds and to gold
I saw the sky-blue car returning like a melody
The lovely lady at the will said: *Hop in, Cassady*

The radio was playing music like I never heard
I didn't have a thing to say, no, not another word
The wheels of the sky-blue car flew down the golden track
The rearview mirror showed nothing that would ever call me back

This is the end of the road
No further passion to unload
Nothing left to do except explode
Here at the end of the road

EVA

You can't outfox—you can't outrace
Guess it's time to turn and face
Miles too big by the looks of it
God knows it may shrink to fit
Blame it on the shifting times
Some are yours; none are mine
I know when I'm lost
don't need a sign

Hey, little Eva—bomp-sh-bomp
Shake that thing and never stop
The boom may fall, the rocks may roll
but, hey, little Eva, I love you so
Hey, little Eva—Hey, little Eva

The dam burst and the flood thereof
swirled through this night of love
As if that wasn't quite enough
we asked some further meaning of . . .
You and I were such a pair
people used to stare
I never could tell from pity
or from envy

Hey, little Eva—bomp-sh-bomp
Shake that thing and never stop
The boom may fall, the rocks may roll
but, hey, little Eva, I love you so
Hey, little Eva—Hey, little Eva

Hey, little Eva,
where do we go from here?
Ain't no use to call for help,
there's no one near
Maybe we should curse or fret,

trust to fate or pray,
or bide awhile in quiet
'cause there's not a lot to say

Hey, little Eva—bomp-sh-bomp
Shake that thing and never stop
The boom may fall, the rocks may roll
but, hey, little Eva, I love you so
Hey, little Eva—Hey, little Eva

Some get wrecked and then complain—
It's their pleasure to show their pain
My little Eva got tears in her eyes
She don't hurt, she just loves to cry
When she really feels the pain
she don't cry at all;
just stands there grinning
with her back against the wall

Hey, little Eva—bomp-sh-bomp
Shake that thing and never stop
The boom may fall, the rocks may roll
but, hey, little Eva, I love you so
Hey, little Eva—Hey, little Eva

EYES OF THE WORLD

Right outside this lazy summer home
you don't have time to call
your soul a critic, no
Right outside the lazy gate
of winter's summer home
wondering where the nuthatch winters
Wings a mile long
just carried
the bird
away

Wake up to find out
that you are the eyes of the world
but the heart has its beaches
its homeland and thoughts
of its own
Wake now, discover that
you are the song that
the morning brings
but the heart has its seasons
its evenings
and songs of its own

There comes a redeemer
and he slowly, too, fades away
There follows a wagon behind him
that's loaded with clay
and the seeds that were silent
all burst into bloom and decay
The night comes so quiet
and it's close on the heels of the day

Wake up to find out
that you are the eyes of the world
but the heart has its beaches

its homeland and thoughts
of its own
Wake now, discover that
you are the song that
the morning brings
but the heart has its seasons
its evenings
and songs of its own

Sometimes we live no
particular way but our own
Sometimes we visit your country
and live in your home
Sometimes we ride on your horses
Sometimes we walk alone
Sometimes the songs that we hear
are just songs of our own

Wake up to find out
that you are the eyes of the world
but the heart has its beaches
its homeland and thoughts
of its own
Wake now, discover that
you are the song that
the morning brings
but the heart has its seasons
its evenings
and songs of its own

FAIR TO EVEN ODDS

How long, Jack, till we get to Singapore?
How long, Joe, did we sign on for?
Better keep bailing while the rain pours down
The day crews sleeping and the night crews
    drowned

Fair to even odds, I wager
Fair to even odds, I lay
If we make it till the sunrise
We can make it through the day

Caught at the border running forty-fives
A shot in the back could mean good-bye
You know I have been shot before
And I didn't lay down and die—no

Fair to even odds, I wager
Fair to even odds, I give
Fair to even I recover
Fair to even odds I live

Lie around and clench my teeth
Until my jaws are sore
Maybe give up cigarettes
Till my lungs don't hurt no more

Shot in the back and drawing flies
Flat on my belly with bloodshot eyes
This is the life I love the best
Devil be welcome to the rest

Fair to even odds, I wager
Fair to even I adore
Away, away, go from my window
Don't you bother me no more

Just how far is this day risen?
Move my head so I can see
Hear the hot sweet winds of Heaven
Thick and red as blood to me

Fair to even odds, I wager
Fair to even odds, I lay
If I make it till the sunrise
I can make it through the day

I can hear the hangman's horn pipe
Blowing high and low and strong
Fare to even odds, dear Annie
Play no sweeter when I'm gone

(The first of several versions was written concurrently with "Friend of the Devil" in 1970.)

FIRE ON THE MOUNTAIN

Long-distance runner, what you standing there for?
Get up, get off, get out of the door
You're playing cold music on the barroom floor
drowned in your laughter and dead to the core
There's a dragon with matches loose on the town
Take a whole pail of water just to cool him down

Fire—Fire on the mountain
Fire—Fire on the mountain

Almost aflame, still you don't feel the heat
Takes all you got just to stay on the beat
You say it's a living, we all gotta eat
but you're here alone, there's no one to compete
If mercy's in business I wish it for you
More than just ashes when your dreams come true

Fire—Fire on the mountain
Fire—Fire on the mountain

Baby's in scarlet, her shackles in gray
If loves to love she's got it salted away
Out of the rat trap and under the wire
Out of the frying pan and into the fire
Put it down heavy, strip it down lean
Got to lay it down dirty and play it back clean

Fire—Fire on the mountain
Fire—Fire on the mountain

Fireman, fireman, call off your dog
this isn't a blaze, it's just a hog in the log
Cut up in sections, squirming alive
lost to the world on that fifty-cent jive
There's a fire on the mountain, running around
what doesn't go up can never come down

Fire—Fire on the mountain
Fire—Fire on the mountain

Long-distance runner, what you holding out for?
Caught in slow motion in your dash to the door
The flame from your stage has now spread to the floor
You gave all you got, why you wanta give more?
The more that you give, why, the more it will take
to the thin line beyond which you really cannot fake

There's a fire
Fire on the mountain
Fire—
Fire on the mountain

(Written at Mickey Hart's ranch in heated inspiration as the surrounding hills blazed and the fire approached the recording studio where we were working; verses three and four don't appear on the Grateful Dead recording of this song, but lines five and six of verse three became one of our mottoes, along with "Record More than You Erase.")

FLETCHER CARNABY

The evil eye of Fletcher Carnaby comes
Lid heavy, his pace is slow
Slow paced, lid heavy and tired
Yes tired, like the beaten-in head of a drum

The evil lines on the face that this man wears
Cannot now be distinguished from the lines of care
Care lined, eyes heavy and tired
Looking for a face from a place no one comes from

Crazy Harry switchblade parking his knife
Shining steel reflects a future wife
Who waits ready, eyes steady as night
Yes steady like only the caved-in can

Sunshine peddlers gather around the block
Eyes as yet unshattered by the rising shock
Quick—ready—lives that are still untried
Untried like the white bitter wine of the moon

(Written in 1973 with Mickey Hart for the *Rolling Thunder* album, this weird little piece is more about internal rhythms than subject matter; intended to function as a kind of voice drum.)

FOOLISH HEART

Carve your name
Carve your name in ice and wind
Search for where
Search for where the rivers end
Or where the rivers start
Do everything that's in you
That you feel to be your part
But never give your love, my friend,
Unto a foolish heart

Leap from ledges
Leap from ledges high and wild
Learn to speak
Speak with wisdom like a child
Directly from the heart
Crown yourself the king of clowns
Or stand way back apart
But never give your love, my friend
Unto a foolish heart

Shun a friend
Shun a brother and a friend
Never look
Never look around the bend
Or check a weather chart
Sign the Mona Lisa
With a spray can, call it art
But never give your love, my friend
Unto a foolish heart

A foolish heart will call on you
To toss your dreams away
Then turn around and blame you
For the way you went astray
A foolish heart will cost you sleep

And often make you curse
A selfish heart is trouble
But a foolish heart is worse

Bite the hand
Bite the hand that bakes your bread
Dare to leap
Where the angels fear to tread
Till you are torn apart
Stoke the fires of paradise
With coals from Hell to start
But never give your love, my friend
Unto a foolish heart

Unto a foolish heart . . .

FOUR WHITE HORSES

When a pistol crack from a bloodshot sky
Picks off each curse you dare to cry
When reason's light by love's dead flame
Shows no one but yourself to blame
When the well is empty if not yet dry
And the thirsty howl if you dare to cry
Bang their cups against your door
To drink your tears till you got no more

Four white horses will carry you home
Clear blue water will flow from stone
Four white horses who step so high,
Swing down low now, bye and bye

When honey pours bitter and sugar turns black
And stings like scratches on a sunburned back
When all things sweet have lost their taste
And a well-meant smile just cracks like paste
When the crow on your cradle prophesies
That the day you're born is the day you die
And you lie there finally cold and dead
In the midnight hour of deepest dread

Four white horses will carry you home
Clear blue water will flow from stone
Four white horses who step so high
Swing down low now, bye and bye

Soon or later all things pass
Four white horses come at last
One from Peter, one from Paul
One from Simon, one from Saul

Four white horses to carry you home
An angel to roll away your stone

Where time ain't nothing but a busted clock
Carry you home, you won't have to walk
Four white horses will carry you home
Clear blue water will flow from stone
Four white horses who step so high
Swing down low now, bye and bye

(This is one of many songs written during a time of deep personal loss. I'll let this necessary statement of hope stand for the rest of them.)

FRANCE

Way down in the south of France
All the ladies love to dance
Kick their heels up in the air
Snap their fingers for romance
While the gentlemen compare
Blond or black or auburn hair
Check the motion and the style
Ah, you know they take their while

To make the motion more complete
Just to make it more a treat
Love will show us where to go
Come on down and see the show
When the rhythm's really right
You can burn it down tonight
When the singing's really fine
Sweet as Spanish sherry wine

When the club can't contain the beat
It just rolls out in the street
Spills on down the avenue
Bringing dancers to their feet
When it's good as it can be
It gets better, wait and see
These folks don't never sleep
Till they're passed out in the street

Way down in the south of France
All the ladies love to dance
Clap their hands and walk on air
Yeah, the feeling's really there
Won't you take a little taste
Raise it to your charming face?
When the rhythm's really right
You can burn it down tonight

When the singing's really fine
Sweet as Spanish sherry wine
Go on, take a chance
The ladies *do* love to dance

★   ★   ★

Sail away from yesterday
Anywhere except tomorrow
Where the people got no heart
Only live to lend and borrow
I don't really need to know
What they've got upon their mind
When they're coming on so low
Never treat each other kind

Hit me easy where I live
I'm no victim to the blues
I just want to stick around
Learn to pick and learn to choose
If you help me through the night
I will try to treat you right
Love me, I will love you, too
Nothing else I'd rather do

Down in the south of France
Ladies do the shadow dance
Kick their feet up in the air
Snap their fingers for romance
While the gentlemen compare
Locks of straight and curly hair
Check the motion and the smile
Sense of rhythm and the style

To make the motion more complete
To sweep the men right off their feet
They leave kisses in the wine
I found one inside of mine
Pass around the loving cup
Drink it down and fill it up
There's enough to go around
Fill it up and drink it down

When the rhythm's really right
You can dance away the night
When the rhythm's really fine
Rare and sweet as vintage wine
Play it on the carousel
Where the ponies run pell-mell
They don't run to get away
They just like to run that way

In the quiet of the night
Does your lover treat you right?
Well, just turn to her and say
Love, I love it just this way
Give her roses, maybe jewels
Learn to play it by the rules
Once you know it's true romance
Go ahead and take a chance

All I really want is you
No one else will really do
Taste of lilac in the air
Scent of perfume in your hair
Sail, oh, sail away with me
Out across the seventh sea
With that silver-dollar moon
And a hurdy-gurdy tune

Down in the south of France
All the ladies love to dance
Clap their hands and walk on air
When the feeling's really there
Make that magic in my heart
From the finish to the start
Never take your love away
It grows sweeter day by day

When the rhythm's really right
You can dance away the night
When the rhythm's really fine
Rare and sweet as vintage wine
Nothing else I'd rather do
Than to spend the night with you
Nothing else I'd rather do
Nothing else I'd rather do

("France" was written to tapes of a joyous afternoon Latin jam at Mickey Hart's ranch, the same jam that spawned "Molly Dee" and "Northeast by West." It was recorded by the Dead with abbreviated lyrics and a very different feel. The first four and a half verses above appear on the album *Shakedown Street*.)

FRANKLIN'S TOWER

In another time's forgotten space
your eyes looked through your mother's face
Wildflower seed on the sand and stone
may the four winds blow you safely home

Roll away . . . the dew
Roll away . . . the dew
Roll away . . . the dew
Roll away . . . the dew

You ask me where the four winds dwell
In Franklin's Tower there hangs a bell
It can ring, turn night to day
Ring like fire when you lose your way

Roll away . . . the dew
Roll away . . . the dew
Roll away . . . the dew
Roll away . . . the dew

God help the child who rings that bell
It may have one good ring left, you can't tell
One watch by night, one watch by day
If you get confused, just listen to the music play

Roll away . . . the dew
Roll away . . . the dew
Roll away . . . the dew
Roll away . . . the dew

Some come to laugh their past away
Some come to make it just one more day
Whichever way your pleasure tends
if you plant ice, you're gonna harvest wind

Roll away . . . the dew
Roll away . . . the dew
Roll away . . . the dew
Roll away . . . the dew

In Franklin's Tower the four winds sleep
Like four lean hounds the lighthouse keep
Wildflower seed in the sand and wind
May the four winds blow you home again

Roll away . . . the dew
Roll away . . . the dew
Roll away . . . the dew
Roll away . . . the dew
You better roll away
the dew. . . .

FRIEND OF THE DEVIL

I lit out from Reno
I was trailed by twenty hounds
Didn't get to sleep that night
Till the morning came around

I set out running but I take my time
A friend of the Devil is a friend of mine
If I get home before daylight
I might get some sleep tonight

I ran into the Devil, babe
He loaned me twenty bills
I spent that night in Utah
In a cave up in the hills

I set out running but I take my time
A friend of the Devil is a friend of mine
If I get home before daylight
I might get some sleep tonight

I ran down to the levee
But the Devil caught me there
He took my twenty-dollar bill
And he vanished in the air

I set out running but I take my time
A friend of the Devil is a friend of mine
If I get home before daylight
I might get some sleep tonight

Got two reasons why I cry
away each lonely night
First one's named sweet Anne Marie
and she's my heart's delight
Second one is prison, baby

the sheriff's on my trail
If he catches up with me
I'll spend my life in jail

Got a wife in Chino, babe
And one in Cherokee
First one says she's got my child
But it don't look like me

I set out running but I take my time
A friend of the Devil is a friend of mine
If I get home before daylight
I might get some sleep tonight

You can borrow from the Devil
You can borrow from a friend
But the Devil will give you twenty
When your friend got only ten

Set out running but I take my time
A friend of the Devil is a friend of mine
If I get home before daylight
I might get some sleep tonight

A GLASS OF WINE AT THE END OF TIME

Nothing but iron
Brick and cement
Blood, detritus
And sentiment

A glass of wine at the end of time
The waves beat grim and slow
A glass of wine at the end of time
Love me love and go

Bells still ring
Clocks can chime
Take your hand
And put it in mine

A glass of wine at the end of time
Stars dripping out of the sky
A glass of wine at the end of time
With my throat so hot and dry

Miles of morning
Acres of night
By noon the sun
Unbearably bright

A glass of wine at the end of time
An old Victrola spins
A glass of wine at the end of time
Where another world begins

What was the promise?
How did we fare?
Will we be mourned?
Does anyone care?

A glass of wine at the end of time
The waves beat grim and slow
A glass of wine at the end of time
Shatter the glass and go

GOLDEN STAIRS

Bet five hundred dollars
Any course you steer
Someone got to argue
Can't get there from here
Easy with that road map
you're flapping in my face
You're a rock-and-roll singer
Not a minister of grace

Go down shining—Go down shine
Go down shining—Shine, shine, shine

Before you sign another loan
To free yourself from debt
Take a careful look around
To see *who* holds the bets
There will be no winners
May not even be a race
Just a lot of starving runners
Staring hunger in the face

Go down shining—Go down shine
Go down shining—Shine, shine, shine

Rock around the Clock again
You got the time to dare
There's never any hurry
When you take it stair by stair
There are no paid vacations
To alleviate the cares
Of the hungry and the homeless
Climbing up the golden stairs

Go down shining—Go down shine
Go down shining—Shine, shine, shine

Go down shining—Go down shine
Go down shining—Shine, shine, shine

Blind and lonesome Hobo
Flag the mystery train
Something that the cat dug up
Dragged in out of the rain
You got all the makings of
A case beyond repair
But you don't need a license
To climb the golden stairs

Go down shining—Go down shine
Go down shining—Shine, shine, shine

Go down shine—Go down shine
Go down shining—Shine, shine, shine

Go down shining—Go down shine
Go down shining—Shine, shine, shine

GOMORRAH

Just a song of Gomorrah
I wonder what they did there
Must of been a bad thing
to get shot down for

I wonder how they blew it up
or if they tore it down
Get out, get out, Mr. Lot
and don't you look around

Who gave you your orders?
Someone from the sky
I heard a voice inside my head
in the desert wind so dry

I heard a voice telling me to flee
The very same voice I always believe
Said: A lot of trouble coming
but it don't have to come to you
I'm sparing you so you can tell
the rest what you been through

But don't you turn around, no
Don't look after you
It's not your business how it's done
You're lucky to get through

You're a good upstanding man
A credit to the flock
But if you don't face straight ahead
You could not take the shock

Blew the city off the map
Left nothing there but fire
The wife of Lot got turned to salt
because she looked behind her

Because she looked behind
Because she looked behind . . .

GREATEST STORY EVER TOLD

Moses came riding up on a guitar
His spurs were a-jingling, the door was ajar
His buckle was silver, his manner was bold
I asked him to come on in out of the cold
His brain was boiling, his reason was spent
He said: *If nothing was borrowed, then nothing was lent*
I asked him for mercy, he gave me a gun
Said: *Now 'n' again these things just got to be done*

Abraham and Isaac
sitting on a fence
You'd get right to work
if you had any sense
Y'know the one thing we need
is a left-hand monkey wrench

Gideon come in with his eyes on the floor
Says: *Y'ain't got a hinge, you can't close the door*
Moses stood up a full six-foot-ten
Says: *You can't close the door when the wall's caved in*
I asked him for water, he poured me some wine
We finished the bottle, then broke into mine
You get what you come for, you're ready to go
It's one in ten thousand just come for the show

Abraham and Isaac
Digging on a well
Mama come quick
with the water-witch spell
Cool clear water
where you can't never tell

(Also known as "Pumpman" and "Moses"—I wrote this to the rhythm of the pump in Mickey Hart's well. In the first line, Bob Weir, who gave the song its present complementary title, sings *quasar* rather than *guitar*.)

THE HANDYMAN RHYME

Alone, apart by the edge of the sand,
shape and sizes fall from our hand;
again and again, without stopping for breath
we finish our lives and surrender to death

Seldom at all unless driven by fear
does anyone hear with the heart of the ear
the song of the handyman hammering hard
to tear down the wall and reveal us

We meet in the wreckage
Find love without fear
but die when our double
steps out of the mirror

You approach by the edge of the sea,
up ahead, I turn, you're behind me—
Do you remember the Handyman's Rhyme?
No I do not—Will you sing it again?

Rap! Tack! Slap of the joiner
Sound of the cutting edge
shearing through pine
Crow on the cradle
Hawk on the table
The first a fable
The second a sign

Run! Quick!
Hide in the mountain

I would run with you
but two cannot pass
I'll hide
deep in the valley
A shadow in shadow
A shade among shades

Stand and deliver
Stumble and fall
Rise! Turn!
Come when I call
From out of the lilac
The roots of the trees
The dew in the morning
The bell in the breeze

You've finished your training
You've learned how to die
Walk me down to the quarry
and kiss me good-bye
Love of my life
We have not loved enough
Our jewels are unpolished
Their settings are rough
I love and release you
Relinquish your line
It's yours now forever
in wishing well time

(This is the oldest song in the book, conceived around 1965 when I lived in the attic of a house where Jerry and Sara Garcia, Dave and Bonnie Parker, Mike O'Connelly, Rick Shubb, David Nelson, Anne Murphy and Neal Cassady all resided sporadically.)

HARP TREE LAMENT

What would it gain me
if I was to go
like Jacob of old
to the well of the world—
to wax halls where candles
burn on through the day
to light you a path
so you'd never lose your way?

I was down in the valley
where shadows are long
The birds in the harp tree
were singing this song:
There is time to deliver
Time to receive
All that you're lacking
of whatever you need

Turn around
bye the bye
You'll still
see the sea
As it was in the dawning
As it always will be

So raise up your glasses
and drink down the blood
You planted the vine here
in spite of the flood
Here's a dram for the piper
and a tune for his lady

Outside the thin walls
the waves are still raging

Here's one for the Harp Tree
and one for his song
One for the morning
when the night was too long
One for the candle that
lights you to bed
And one for the sword
that hangs over your head

(This little song resides on a fine and all but overlooked pre-Starship album by BARON VON TOLLBOOTH AND THE CHROME NUN by Grace Slick, Paul Kantner, and David Freiberg, who wrote the melody and sang it. The title is taken from a piobaireachd for Highland pipe.)

HELP ON THE WAY

Paradise waits
on the crest of a wave
her angels in flame
She has no pain
Like a child, she is pure
She is not to blame

Poised for flight
Wings spread bright
Spring from night
into the sun
Don't stop to run
She can fly like a lie
She cannot be outdone

Tell me the cost
I can pay
Let me go
Tell me love is not lost
Sell everything
Without love, day to day,
insanity's king

I will pay
day by day
anyway
Lock, bolt, and key
Crippled but free
I was blind
all the time
I was learning to see

Help on the way
I know only this
I've got you today

Don't fly away
'cause I love what I love
and I want it that way

I will stay
one more day
Like I say
Honey, it's you
Without love in the dream
It will never come true

HERE COMES SUNSHINE

Wake of the flood
laughing water
'49
Get out the pans
don't just stand there dreaming
get out the way

Here comes sunshine
. . .here comes sunshine!

Line up a long shot
Maybe try it two times
Maybe more
Good to know
you got shoes to wear
when you find the floor
Why hold out for more?

Here comes sunshine
. . . here comes sunshine!

Asking you nice now
keep the mother rolling
one more time
Been down before
but you just don't have to
go no more

Here comes sunshine
. . . here comes sunshine!

(Remembering the great Vanport, Washington flood of 1949, living in other people's homes, a family
abandoned by father; second grade)

HE'S GONE

Rat in a drain ditch
Caught on a limb
You know better but
I know him
Like I told you
What I said
Steal your face
right off you head

Now he's gone
Lord, he's gone
Like a steam locomotive
rolling down the track
He's gone
He's gone
and nothing's gonna bring him back
He's gone

Nine-mile skid
on a ten-mile ride
Hot as a pistol
but cool inside
Cat on a tin roof
Dogs in a pile
Nothing left to do but
smile, smile, smile

Now he's gone
Lord, he's gone
Like a steam locomotive
rolling down the track
He's gone
He's gone
and nothing's gonna bring him back
He's gone

Going where the wind don't blow so strange
Maybe on some high cold mountain range
Lost one round but the price wasn't anything
Knife in the back and more of the same
Same old rat in a drain ditch
Out on a limb
You know better but I know him

Now he's gone
Lord, he's gone
Like a steam locomotive
rolling down the track
He's gone
He's gone
and nothing's gonna bring him back
He's gone. . .

HIGH TIME

You told me good-bye
How was I to know
You didn't mean good-bye
You meant *please*
don't let me go
I was having a high time
living the good life
Well, I know

The wheels are muddy
Got a ton of Hay
Now listen here, baby
'cause I mean what I say
I'm having a hard time
living the good life
Well, I know

I was losing time
I had nothing to do
No one to fight
I came to you
Wheels broke down
The leader won't draw
The line is busted
the last one I saw

Tomorrow come trouble
Tomorrow come pain
Now don't think too hard, baby
'cause you know what I'm saying
I could show you a high time
living the good life
Don't be that way

Nothing's for certain
It could always go wrong
Come in when it's raining
Go on out when it's gone
We could have us a high time
living the good life
Well, I know

HOLLYWOOD CANTATA

Hollywood is everywhere you go
Move on in before you lose your glow
Always first in line when you're the show
Trick or treat got nothing to compare
Million-dollar daydreams end up there

Naked virgin starlet saints in love
Fit each other just like hand in glove
Waiting for that message on the phone
Misery when hope drops like a stone
Long and low like K.C. mighta moan

Hollywood is everywhere
Graceful children walk on air
Get down on it when you should
And you'll get by in Hollywood

Sunrise over Sunset, yes, indeed
Hollywood is all you let it be
Wait awhile, just hang in there and see
Everyone's got someone else's price
All they want is just another slice

Look at Margo, tell me: Can she move
In those knock-me-down-and-kick-me shoes?
Gets her feet right down inside the groove
Hollywood is everywhere she go
Spread out from the high heels to the low

Hollywood is everywhere
Graceful children walk on air
If you don't get down when you should
You'll never get to Hollywood

Plain to see you don't fit anywhere
Stand up, someone sure to grab your
    chair
Is this a tail or just the dog it wags
Packed so tight it hardly ever sags
Dips its heart in dime and nickel bags

Don't let your heart be the one she
    breaks
She don't allow a lover two mistakes
Don't let your heart be the one she
    breaks
She don't allow a lover two mistakes
Don't let your heart be the one she
    breaks

Hollywood is everywhere
Graceful children walk on air
If you don't move down there for good
You'll never make it in Hollywood

(Unused lyrics I wrote to some rudimentary changes by Bob Weir that eventually became "The Music Never Stopped," by Weir and John Barlow)

HOLY BROOKLYN CROWN

They sprang from the alley with razors in hand
Fought back to back in a tight little band
From tenement windows, a wife looking down
Roar of the subway drowns most of the sound

Under the shadow of Brooklyn Bridge
It's all coming down
Broken bones and bullet holes
For the Holy Brooklyn Crown

Steam heat struggles through inches of rust
Where Marie and her child look down in disgust
He looks like his old man below on the street,
A chain in his hand beating someone to meat

Call out the law
Maybe she should
But nothing stops for them
The cops slow down
Shine their lights
Speed on off again

She's seen a lot of young men in her time
Crippled or jailed or dead in their prime
She's ready to walk, but where can she go?
Back to the window to look down below

Suddenly the dark is split
The night lit up like fire
The Brooklyn Bridge has turned to gold
And angels sing in choir

There stands a Madonna with robes glowing blue
Our Lady of Brooklyn with glory shot through
Who blesses the child who was born to the street
Where Marie's man is falling but still on his feet

Under the shadow of Brooklyn Bridge
The final trumpet sounds
The prowl car blows its siren
This time it don't slow down

A dark cloud rolls 'cross the face of the moon
There is silence except for a jukebox tune
A party of drunks from a bar shutting down
Plays kick-the-can with the Brooklyn Crown

(Written to the same Freiberg changes as "Book of Daniel," on "Jack O' Roses")

HOOKER'S BALL

Where you gonna be when midnight falls?
Honey, I'll be at the Hooker's Ball
Where you gonna be around two o'clock?
Back on Leavenworth walkin' the block

Walk, walk
Walk, walk
Walkin' the block
ah-oo, walk
walk, walk
Walkin' the block

What you gonna say when they haul you in?
Don't say nothin', never say nothin'
What you gonna say when you're free again?
Don't say nothin', go high-struttin'

Walk, walk
Walk, walk
Walkin' the block
ah-oo, walk
walk, walk
Walkin' the block

I'll take Margo and you take Jane
We're both good-lookin' but we ain't the same
Honey, where'd you learn to talk that talk?
Down on Haight Street walkin' the block

Walk, walk
Walk, walk
Walkin' the block
ah-oo, walk
walk, walk
Walkin' the block

Where you gonna be when midnight falls?
Honey, I'll be at the Hooker's Ball
Where you gonna be 'round two o'clock?
Back on Scott Street walkin' the block

Walkin' the block, ooh
Walkin' the block
Walk, walk
Walk, walk
Walkin' the block
ah-oo, walk
walk, walk
Walkin' the block

(The official theme song for the final Hooker's Ball in 1978. The San Francisco city council decided such an annual event was unseemly and refused to rent its Brook's Hall facility to Margo St. James's COYOTE prostitutes' support group anymore. A commercial venture called the Exotic Erotic Ball has taken its place and seems to be okay with them.)

IF I HAD THE WORLD TO GIVE

If I had the world to give
I'd give it to you—long as you live
Would you let it fall
or hold it all in your arms?

If I had a song to sing
I'd sing it to you—as long as you live
Lullaby—or maybe a plain serenade
wouldn't you laugh, dance, and cry
or be afraid at the trade you made?

I may not have the world to give to you
but maybe I have a tune or two
Only if you let me be your world
could I ever give this world to you
could I ever give this world to you

But I will give what love I have to give
I will give what love I have to give
I will give what love I have to give
long as I live

If I had a star to give
I'd give it to you—long as you live
Would you have the time
to watch it shine—watch it shine
or ask for the moon and heaven, too?
I'd give it to you

Maybe I've got no star to spare
or anything fine or even rare
Only if you let me be your world
would I ever give this world to you
could I ever give this world to you

I HEARD YOU SINGING

I heard you singing
What were you singing when the people got right?
Were you singing *Stand and Deliver?*
Or was it *Down by the River?*
Were you singing a fine old tune like *Gone to Glory?*
Laying it down with grace and power
Long about the midnight hour
I heard the people all singing
Like they'd never sung before
All over the country
Who could help but stand beside you?

Hello, hello—is there anybody here?
My knuckles are sore from rapping all day
I said: Give me one more chance
I'd do it for you if I had your way . . . if I had your way

What do I know? What do I see?
Don't know nothing but the name of the game
It's high-card draw with everything wild
You bet your life like anyone's child
What else would you want to do?

I heard the people all singing
Like they never sung before
Singing in key and strumming
Everything they heard from you
Hello, hello, hello, hello . . . good-bye

Looking back across the years
Other matters disappear
In the murmur I can hear
Familiar voices loud and clear
Hello, hello, hello, hello . . . good-bye

I heard you singing
Like one last song in the middle of night
Were you singing in tongues of fire
Or was it knots of anger?

Were you singing a fine old tune like
Love Me, Love Me, Love Me Only?
Were you caught between the curtains
Thinking this was too uncertain?

Remember . . . the people were singing
Like they never sung before
All over the country
Did you love the way they loved you?

Ain't no knocker on the last big door
Just push on the panel and walk on in
Hello, hello, is there anybody here
But a two-bit high and a busted mirror?
Hello, hello—is anybody here?
My tongue is so sore from rapping all day

Sunshine in the dead of night . . .
I know that can't be right
Could it be? I don't know
But it never done that thing before
So close to my own back door
It got me wondering what to do
And the only thing was to come and tell you
because—I heard you singing—I heard you

IN A LOVE DREAM

From your cellar door to a star
Never so high or so far
Just to be where you are
Let me be where you are
In a love dream
Love dream

Oh my Love, to leave you alone
Never to see you come home
Won't turn me to stone
But how the cold winds moan
In a love dream
Love dream

Save me the rose of October
Winter is coming and all
Tell me the dream is not over
If only you'd come when I call
In a love dream
Love dream

You cannot be taken from me
No, never from me
That's what it means to believe
And all it means to believe
In a love dream
Love dream

Look from the top of the steeple
Abraham, Isaac and me
Oh such helpless people
How can such helpless ones be
In a love dream?
Love dream

You cannot be taken from me
No, no, never from me
Long as I choose to believe
Long as I need to believe

In a love dream
Love dream

From your cellar door to a star
Never so high or so far
Just to be where you are
Help me to be where you are
In a love dream
Love dream

INDEPENDENCE DAY

If you can't recollect the larger picture
maybe you should step back for perspective
You might swear all promise is rejected
and you can't tell what move might be effective
It's not like a major revolution
and there were no tables firmly turned around
though you might have thought there were in the confusion
My God, you would of sworn it from the sound

All you know is it's
Not like Independence Day
No, it's not like Independence Day
With the flags that wave and the bands that play
No, it's not like Independence Day

You might have heard the ongoing singer
You must have heard the ongoing song
You will admit the time was never riper
You can see without much sight how far it's gone
And it isn't only matters
that were settled long ago
And it isn't just the singer
and it wasn't just a show

All you know is it's
Not like Independence Day
No, it's not like Independence Day
With the flags that wave and the bands that play
No, it's not like Independence Day

Perhaps you remember Jack the Jester
Got so high he tried to milk the cat
The damned thing turned around and scratched his eyes out
Could be a lesson for all of us in that
If it wasn't what you ordered
Would you eat it anyway?
Would you waste the time to close the barn door
after your pig, your cow, your chickens, and your tractor have all flown away?

Just say bye-bye
baby blackbird
just say bye-bye, bye-bye, bye-bye, bye-bye

'Cause it's not like Independence Day
No, though it might be a little
like Happy New Year
But it's not like Independence Day
with all those shooting stars
and the bands that play
No, it's not like Independence Day with
Thomas Jefferson singing *Not Fade Away*
No, it's not like Independence Day

I NEVER SEE YOU

Put the load in the wagon
Put the wagon on the road
not the weight on me
I'm cut down in my tracks
My back is killing me
Looking at the picture
from all directions
including through
Does it still amaze?
Boy, you know it never
will cease to do
But all that aside
it's been a long time
    I never see you
    How come I never do?

Tie the tackle to the line
put the line to the rod
not the hook in me
Weigh your words
Throw your light on the page
not the book at me
I was just sitting here doing
what I thought I was
supposed to do
Looked up in surprise
there was nobody left
not even you
    Tell me, do
    why
    I never see you
    How come I never do?

Pour the drop in the bucket
Put the bucket in the tub
not the rub on me
I got trouble enough
without coming to grips
with reality

So what if I traded some
empty chatter for solitude?
You know I still come around
when I'm in the mood
    but when I do
    I never see you
    How come I never do?

The other day I was talking at length
to a friend of yours
who told me I really should come around
it would open a lot of doors
In due course I came around
the doors were open wide
on the same old empty rooms
Neither you nor your friend were inside
    Could you tell me why
    I never see you
    How come I never do?

Put the horse on the track
Put your cash on his back
not the flak on me
You do what you do
or don't
in spite of the lack of me
I get where I'm going as fast in the back
as in the driver's seat
and I don't get left out holding the bag
down on lonely street
although we meet—occasionally
    I never see you
    How come I never do?
    I never see you

I T

I got a letter and the postage was due
I never shoulda read it but returned it to you
I never got such a dumb letter before
Ain't gonna read 'em, don't send me no more
Here's a map to the kitchen, a ticket to the door
Got enough trouble, not looking for more, thanks

It, it
What can it be?
It, it, it, it
Fooling with me

I read in your letter that my business had failed
Then I read my mother had escaped from jail
Lookin' me up, she thinks I put her in
Gonna lay me flat with a rollin' pin
My turtle and my goldfish have committed suicide
Now you tell me to take it all in my stride, thanks

It, it
What can it be?
It, it, it, it
Fooling with me

Maybe I'll get it before it gets me
Maybe I'll regret it, I'll chance it and see
Maybe I'll forget it until it comes due
then pay the penalty and the interest, too
Maybe I'll claim it on what I deduct
which they might not allow
It all depends on my luck

It, it
What can it be?
It, it, it, it
Fooling with me

I had a friend who got *it* on his shoe
He laid the blame on me, I tried to lay it on you
You laid it on another, just a bump on the log
No one ever thought to lay it on the dog
Now I'm just sitting here sad as can be
wondering what *it*'s got in store for me

It, it
What can it be?
It, it, it, it
Fooling with me

IT MUST HAVE BEEN THE ROSES

Annie laid her head down in the roses
She had ribbons, ribbons, ribbons
in her long brown hair
I don't know, it must have been the roses
All I know is I could not leave her there

I don't know
it must have been the roses
The roses or the ribbons
in her long brown hair
I don't know
maybe it was the roses
All I know was
I could not leave her there

Ten years the waves rolled the
ships home from the sea
Thinking well how it may blow
in all good company
if I tell another what
your own lips told to me
may I lay 'neath the roses
and my eyes no longer see

I don't know
it must have been the roses
The roses or the ribbons
in her long brown hair
I don't know
maybe it was the roses
All I know was
I could not leave her there

One pane of glass in the window
No one is complaining, though,

come in and shut the door
Faded is the crimson from the
ribbons that she wore
and it's strange how no one
comes round anymore

I don't know
it must have been the roses
The roses or the ribbons
in her long brown hair
I don't know
maybe it was the roses
All I know was
I could not leave her there

Annie laid her head down in the roses
She had ribbons, ribbons, ribbons
in her long brown hair
I don't know, it must have been the roses
All I know was I could not leave her there

IT'S ONLY MUSIC

Don't look too far
You can find it everywhere
You can lose it without a warning
If you grab on too tight
Or try to read too much into it
You know it's only music—

That song—that song
The one you hear inside at night
It can set you reeling—that song
Is just your own heart beating
But it can sound like a symphony—

You hear a voice so clear
You can't tell what it's saying
Well maybe you know
That tune you hear
Might never end—

I thought that I heard you singing
    at night
You know I had the feeling
That I have heard that song
Way beyond this life without beginning—

Who knows the name of that song?
Go broke and come back singing
Since the world appeared
Can't write it down
'Cause it doesn't spell
And it doesn't end—

In the still—in the still of the night
When the wind is quiet—quiet and still
I sit inside the empty room
And wait to hear the tune

That comes stealing through the mazes
Writ on empty pages—

Well I know we'll never get that song
    quite right
But still we're singing
Well I know ten thousand tunes are
    captured there
That much I know—

Blue sun under the clouds
The smoke of wrack and ruin
Someone waits beneath the roses
Playing guitar—playing for me—
Where I don't see—

Don't look too far
You can find it most anywhere
But you can lose it without a warning
If you grab on too tight
Try to read too much into it
You know it's only music—
Don't try too hard
It will come to you
Yes it will

(This tune, music by David Freiberg, appears on Grace Slick's 1973 solo album *Manhole* and is set to the same changes as *I Heard You Singing,* which song appears on both *Tales of the Great Rumrunners* and Quicksilver's final album *Solid Silver.* Freiberg and I got value for money out of these flexible changes.)

JACK STRAW

We can share the women
We can share the wine
We can share what we got of yours
'Cause we done shared all of mine

Keep a-rolling
Just a mile to go
Keep on rolling, my old buddy
You're moving much too slow

I just jumped the watchman
Right outside the fence
Took his ring, four bucks in change
Now ain't that heaven-sent?

Hurts my ears to listen, Shannon
Burns my eyes to see
Cut down a man in cold blood, Shannon
Might as well be me

We used to play for silver
Now we play for life
One's for sport and one's for blood
At the point of a knife
Now the die is shaken
Now the die must fall
There ain't a winner in this game
Who don't go home with all
Not with all . . .

Leaving Texas
Fourth day of July
Sun so hot, clouds so low
The eagles filled the sky

Catch the Detroit Lightning
Out of Santa Fe
Great Northern out of Cheyenne
From sea to shining sea

Gotta get to Tulsa
First train we can ride
Got to settle one old score
And one small point of pride . . .

Ain't no place a man can hide, Shannon
Keep him from the sun
Ain't no bed will give us rest, man,
You keep us on the run

Jack Straw from Wichita
Cut his buddy down
Dug for him a shallow grave
And laid his body down

Half a mile from Tucson
By the morning light
One man gone and another to go
My old buddy, you're moving much too slow

We can share the women
We can share the wine . . .

JACOB BAUM (WATER WITCH)

I dug in that spot before, I didn't find no water
Tell me, how do *you* do it, where did you get that power?
I got it from my father, who was a seventh son
Don't really need no willow wand, though I guess it helps me some

Water witch, come now
Bend your willow and see
Is there water in my land?
Cool, sweet water for me?
Find that water now, cold clear water
Flow from an underground spring
Come, cool water—Oh, come, sweet water
Please bend your willow and see

Jacob Baum came to Nehi Valley nineteen forty and nine
All the wells were long gone dry—heaven presented no sign
Jacob could sniff a hidden spring like a hound can track a scent
Water never failed to show wherever his willow bent

Preacher Will got it in his head that Jacob was the devil
Said no one could do this thing and still be on the level
During the controversy Jacob dowsed the chapel ground
Found a mother wellspring there, enough to go around

It so happened that Preacher Will, he owned that plot of land
Got it on a deed of trust from someone lately damned
You should have seen his colors change—his true concern turned
  'round
To how much he could profit from the water inside his ground

Water witch, come now
Bend your willow and see
Is there water in my land?
Cool, sweet water for me?
Find that water now, cold clear water
Flow from an underground spring
Come, cool water—Oh, come, sweet water
Please bend your willow and see

Everyone saw through his scam to profit from disaster
Nonetheless, our hands were tied, our need made him the master
Till Jacob shook his willow wand in anger at the sky
And rain fell down for seven days till not one well was dry

Preacher Will snuck out of town the day the sun returned
We took up a collection to pay Jacob what he'd earned
He said: *I can't accept your pay or my power will be lost*
Thank you for your faith in me—that's all it's gonna cost

Water witch, come now
Bend your willow and see
Is there water in my land?
Cool, sweet water for me?
Find that water now, cold clear water
Flow from an underground spring
Come, cool water—Oh, come, sweet water
Please bend your willow and see

Come, cold water—come, cool, sweet water
Jacob, bend your willow and see
Witch that water, now, cold clear water
Cool, sweet water for me. . .

JESSE JAMES

I come here to pass the time
To court the ladies and taste the wine
Jesse James from Abilene
Where do you think they're gonna lay me?

Down under
Under the ground
Way down under the ground

Got one old hat and two old shoes
Come here, sweet Mama, 'cause I got the blues
I been thinking 'bout all that I see
One of these days they're gonna lay me

Down under
Under the ground
Way down under the ground

You sit down 'cause I'm gonna sing
If you like my song I might buy the drinks
I see by your smile you're the salt of the land
Keep your paws on the table while I deal your hand

Down under
Under the ground
Way down under the ground

Ashes to ashes and dust to dust
You look like a man that I can trust
Robert Ford, you're my good friend
I got bread and a bed to lend

You can call me Howard
But it ain't my name
The people all know me
As Jesse James

And there ain't no man with
    the
law in his hand
can track me down in
this whole land

You can call me Howard
But it ain't my name
Everybody knows
That I'm Jesse James

Down under
Under the ground
Way down under the ground
Down under
Under the ground
You put me
Way down under the ground

JOHNNY BLONDINO

In the middle of the ocean
On a boat without a sail
A broken rudder in my hand
And an empty drinking pail
The sun pours down like madness
From a bright and cloudless sky
Staring down into my soul
With a cruel unblinking eye

Johnn . . . y Blondino
A thousand miles from shore
Bill . . . y Blondino
Oh hear the ocean roar

Companions lay around me
A ghastly lifeless horde
Got no strength to lift 'em up
And drop 'em overboard
Thick and fast the visions come
Both kindly and insane
Welling up like mercy
From the fever in my brain

Johnn . . . y Blondino . . . etc.

I have lived a checkered life
Good deeds were far and few
Always counted on my wits
And luck to pull me through
That don't come to no account
When wits and luck are dead
And all the shadows of the past
Come swimming through my head

Johnn . . . y Blondino

I saw the girl I used to love
And the girl I left behind
The girl I sometimes dream about
And the girl that's on my mind
They did a dance together
In a circle round the boat
And sang a song I clearly heard
With neither word nor note

Johnn . . . y Blondino

I found an old harmonica
In someone's salty shirt
I bit my lips to bring the blood
And played until it hurt
I guess it was some kind of prayer
That called out from my pain
Before my lips exploded
It started in to rain

Johnn . . . y Blondino
A thousand miles from shore
Bill . . . y Blondino
Oh hear the ocean roar

JUST ANOTHER TRAIN

Just another train
Just another track
Just another lover
who won't be back

Just another lover
leaving in the night
One more affair that
didn't work out right

Just another pity
Just another shame
Just another alibi
Like more of the same

Just another case
of the hard-luck tale
Like as not it
all ends in jail

I don't want to hear it
I don't want to know
I know that story
from long ago

Don't need to hear it
I've heard it enough
Another girl crying
It's the same old stuff

Back in Sioux City twenty years ago
Papa left Mama, woah didn't he, though?
Seven years later, give or take four
He showed up again at Mama's front door

Mama, kind woman, took him by the hand
Said: Sit yourself down upon the new divan
Good gracious, you look like a different man
There's a couple of things you got to understand

This is your namesake, he's eight
    years old
Here's little Lily, now hasn't she
    growed?
Here's another one you haven't
    yet met
who belongs to my husband, now
    you better get

Catch another train, burn up an-
    other track
This is one of those places you
    can't come back
Just another train—just another
    track
Now just get rolling—and don't
    come back

KEEP THE WATCH

Keep the watch through the daytime
Keep the watch through the night
Keep the watch when you are weary
And nothing comes out right

Keep the watch with one another
Keep the watch when others go
Keep the watch when they all tell you
That there's nothing left to know

Keep the watch, O you children
Through the dawn's early light
When the sun sets on the mountain
Keep the watch through the night

Keep the watch when you are lied to
Keep the watch when you're deceived
Keep the watch when you are shut out
Keep the watch when you're received

Keep the watch when you are baffled
Keep the watch when you are lamed
Keep the watch when you are set up
Keep the watch when you are blamed

Keep the watch, O you children
Through the dawn's early light
When the sun sets on the mountain
Keep the watch through the night

Keep the watch when you are shattered
Keep the watch when you are lost
Keep the watch as though it mattered
Even when you're double-crossed

Keep the watch when you are frazzled
Keep the watch when you are cool
Keep the watch when you are dazzled
And made to look the fool

Keep the watch, O you children
Through the dawn's early light
When the sun sets on the mountain
Keep the watch through the night

Keep the watch inside the darkness
Keep the watch till night is o'er
Keep the watch, O sweet children
Till you can watch no more

Keep the watch through pain and sorrow
Keep the watch through desperate night
Keep the watch until tomorrow
And on through the morning light

Keep the watch, O you children
Till you can watch no more
Keep the watch until you finally see
What you've been watching for

KEEP YOUR DAY JOB

Maybe you collect or maybe you pay
Still got to work that eight-hour day
Whether you like that job or not
Gotta do your work while you're
lining up your long shot
Which is to say
hey–ey

Keep your day job
Don't give it away
Keep your day job
Whatever they say

Ring that bell for whatever it's worth
When Monday comes don't forget about work
By now you know that face on your dollar
got a thumb to its nose and a
hand on your collar
Which is to say
hey–ey

Keep your day job
Don't give it away
Keep your day job
Whatever they say

Punch that time card
Check that clock
When Monday comes
You gotta run, run, run
Not walk

Keep your day job
Don't give it away
Keep your day job
Whatever they say

Steady, boy, study that eight-day hour
but don't underrate that paycheck power

If you ask me, which I know you don't,
I'd tell you to do what I know you won't
Which is to say
hey-ey

Keep your day job
Don't give it away
Keep your day job
Whatever they say
Keep your day job
Until your night job pays

(This song was dropped from the Grateful Dead repertoire at the request of fans. Seriously.)

KEYS TO THE RAIN

Hammer and ripsaw, the waves keep a-risin'
Step up and tell us the name of your poison
I took a step forward, fell out of my hat
at the sign in the window saying "Take What You Lack"
I went to inquire just about how much pain
was needed to purchase the keys to the rain
I mean, who do you think is gonna believe it
when you tell 'em you got the keys to the rain?

Sweet Mary was walking her dog in the fire
singing some tune called "My Hope and Desire"
Her tears were like needles that hung on a chain
She didn't ask nothing 'cept more of the same
Her blue eye was scarlet, her blind eye was fame
She wore a tattoo that read "Lock Up the Rain,"
I mean, who do you ever get to believe it
when you tell 'em you got the keys to the rain?

Yo no soy marinero, por tú seré
por te serai, por tú seré
Para bailar a La Bamba
se necesita un poco de gracia

The prodigal son steals off in the night
He done it before and it worked out all right
He took a wrong turning, wound up in a ditch
He coulda done worse, though, and ended up rich
His songs were cut open and found to be clay
The hope of the future served up on a tray
I mean, who do you think is gonna believe it
when you tell 'em you got the keys to the rain?

You caught me and held me and called me your own
Then kicked in my teeth and left with my bone
Now I know you ain't little but I ain't that small
and you had surprise on your side, after all
So I'm making a wish, I never done that before
This is the first time and I hope there ain't more

But just who do you think you're gonna get to believe you
when you tell 'em you got the keys to the rain?

The just and the crippled both push up the flowers
and nothing remains but the song of the hours
I hope you can dig it, I know that you will
but please don't run hide when I come with my bill
And before you get trying this noose on for size
it's so quick to fall, yes, and so slow to rise—
And who do you think you ever get to believe it
when you tell 'em you got the keys to the rain?
Yeah, who do you think is gonna believe it
when you tell 'em you got the keys to the rain?

KICK IN THE HEAD

Do you think we can work it on out?
Change the whole proposition about?
I'm in no position for an act of sedition
but I really love to scream and shout

Half a loaf is better than a kick in the knee
Is there gonna be some tea or just more sympathy?
I really got a pumper on the line this time
and it's mine, mine, mine

I ran to the King of Creation
I told him: Save a bit for me
The way things look I could have written the book
and you know I can't hardly read

Sally, does your dog bite?
No, no, no
Keep him on a choke chain
Reel him out slow
Got a little place
Call it my own
It never really was a home
No, no, no, no, no

Went to the College of Evil
The smoke nearly drove me away
I'd go crazy if I wasn't so lazy
What more can I say?

White-face Lydian judge
won't you give a little one-two-three?
Him down on the corner singing "Little Jack Horner"
but you got to let the gravy be

A whole loaf is better than a kick in the head
Tell me what you mean, I'll tell you what you said
I sent you for jelly, you come back with jam
Who exactly do you think I am?

Who do you
think I am?
Who do you
think I am?
Just another kick
Just another kick
Just another kick in the head?

(Dave Torbert used to sing this with the New Riders, and I did it with both Roadhog and the Dinosaurs.
It was a lot of fun to sing, but always made me hoarse, for which reason I had to drop it from my repertoire.)

KICK IT ON DOWN

One more midnight haul to the break of day
Bon temps to roll on—what do you say?
Just live once, so what the heck
We did it up and payed the check
Say, babe, hey, now, didn't we

Kick it on down
Kick it on down
Kick it on down, down, down
Watch out!
Oh, what a night out on the town
We set 'em up and we knocked 'em down
Say, babe, hey, now, didn't we?

Always the first to come and the last to go
Didn't we do it, Mama, didn't we, though?
Didn't take time to mess around
We gave as good as we ever found
Say, babe, hey, now, didn't we

Kick it on down
Kick it on down
Kick it on down, down, down
Watch out!
Oh, what a night out on the town
We set 'em up and we knocked 'em down
Say, babe, hey, now, didn't we?

Signed an IOU the day we met
Pay up when it's due with no regret
Burned our bridges one by one
But we crossed 'em when it's said and done
Hey, babe, say, now, didn't we

Kick it on down
Kick it on down
Kick it on down, down, down
Watch out!

Oh, what a night out on the town
We set 'em up and we knocked 'em
    down
Say, babe, hey, now, didn't we?

Gonna do it up, babe, while we can
Ask nobody's leave—don't give a
    damn
Did it up and we did it well
Just live once, so what the hell
Say, babe, hey, now, didn't we

Kick it on down
Kick it on down
Kick it on down, down, down
Watch out!
Oh, what a night out on the town
We set 'em up and we knocked 'em
    down
Say, babe, hey, now, didn't we?

LADY SIMPLICITY

Lady Simplicity
Bright like a ribbon bow
Everything everywhere
Just for the show
Believe it implicitly
Love is tranquility
If you don't know that
Then nothing is known

(I laid down sixteen tracks of stacked vocals on the recording of this nursery rhyme, which opens my first solo album.)

LAST FLASH OF ROCK AND ROLL

Late last night, going insane
I tore out smokin' in the pourin' rain
I tuned into K-Jam Jelly Roll
They got a little less talk
and a little more soul
I thought I heard Laura
—or was it Bette?—
Singing "Nearer My God but Not Just Yet"
Singing "Blue, Blue, Am I Blue?"
You nearly blew me down!
I heard "Long Tall Sally" in terminal pain
Then they played the Rolling Stones again!

It was the last flash of rock and roll
A jack-beat boogie with a two-stroke roll
Last flash of rock and roll
Catch it quick 'cause it rolls along
Last flash/Last flash
Last flash/Last flash of rock and roll

Heard "Who Do You Hate?" and "Who Do You Love?"
Heard "Tired of Countin' the Stars Above"
My own voice singing screams profane
It was four on the floor in the driving rain
The way they lay you get just one chance
Pick it up, Baby, learn to dance
Go for gold, you can go for broke
but don't go for dreams that go up in smoke
Love's to love, not to hold
It's been said before but it's never been told
You can say it right or say it wrong
but it's got to be the heart of a rock-and-roll song

That's the last flash of rock and roll
A true fine mama with a heart of gold
It never was new and it will never grow old
That's your last flash of rock and roll
Last flash/Last flash
Last flash/Last flash

Play it loud, you can play it long
Turn it off or you can turn it on
Save it up or you could use it now
with a thousand singers all tellin' you how
to trip on your fancy—to trip on your feet
trip the light fantastic right down to the street
With a back-beat boogie you can never lose
we tell one another what we all can use

That's the last flash of rock and roll
A jack-beat boogie with a two-stroke roll
It never was new and it will never grow old
That's your last flash of rock and roll
Last flash/Last flash
Last flash/that's the last flash

Saw you grinnin' in the magazine
making all the parties and the rock-and-roll scenes
You blew the words and you called it soul
but we all fall a little short of rock and roll
Step up closer, see what you get
A little nearer to thee but not just yet
Singing "Blue, Blue—Am I Blue?"
You nearly blew me down!
I heard "Long Tall Sally" in terminal pain
Then they played the Rolling Stones again!

It was the last flash of rock and roll
It was a true fine mama with a heart of gold
It never was new, it'll never grow old
That's your last flash of rock and roll

LAUGHING IN THE DARK

What do you have to offer
But a shopworn alibi
Telling how you come to laugh
When maybe you should cry
Or how you come to vanish
When the celebration starts
Then stroll back through the ashes
Like some king of broken hearts?

Roll until you rumble
Like the hoofbeats of a race
Roll until you crumble
And dissolve without a trace
Roll until you stutter
Roll until you spark
In spite of all those hollow voices
Laughing in the dark

What do you have to offer
But a way to waste my time
And a twisted sense of humor
When our lives are on the line?
I believe in something better
And hope it turns out true
But I won't stoop to prophesy
Or believe it when *you* do

Roll until you rumble . . .

Is this all you've got to offer
Is this where you sign your name?
Sketching lonely faces
On a foggy window pane
When the fog is lifted
And the faces disappear

Look how far you've drifted
From the things that seemed so near

I saw you coming to me
And I thought I heard you say
"When today becomes tomorrow
They call it yesterday . . .
All the things you cherish
Down deep inside your heart
Are doomed by contradiction
And just have to blow apart"

Roll for ever higher stakes
And break those aces twice
It's not an easy point to throw
But worth the sacrifice
If you fade, you lose a turn
But while you win, you roll
If you don't gain a pardon
Well, you still might win parole

Roll until you rumble
Like the hoofbeats of a race
Roll until you crumble
And dissolve without a trace
Roll until you stutter
Roll until you spark
In spite of all those hollow voices
Laughing in the dark

LAY OF THE SUNFLOWER

I must leave you for a season
Go out logging that hardwood timber
Hardwood timber that grows so low
In the forest of Fennario

Tell me what you need to live, love
Do you ask that you might own
Keep my blue-eyed hound to guard you
I will make my way alone

I will not return in winter
If I be not back by fall
Seek me when this small sunflower
Stands above the garden wall

Fare you well and I would not weep
Bid you tend your prayers to keep
Hill by dale now must I go
To the forest of Fennario

Nine-month blew with sleeted rain
And still he came not back again
Summoned she the hound to go
To seek him in Fennario

He came back the fated day
To find his lady gone away
Made haste to follow in her track
Where she could go but not turn back

The blue-eyed hound at her side did bay
While fast her breath did fade away
She cried out: *Turn, my love, and go*
I would not have you see me so

I shall not turn, I shall not yield
Oh, selfsame serpent sting my heel
That bleeds my lady's blood away
Beside the blue-eyed hound to lay

Angels sing their souls to sleep
Four winds grace their breath to keep
Up above yon garden wall
Stands the sunflower, straight and tall

LAZY TIGER RAG

Cucuburu Boogie and Coatamundi Cakewalk
Lazy Tiger Rag moving easy to a slow rock
Don't know how to do it?
There could be a reason why
I never taught you how but
now I'm gonna try

Lazy Tiger Rag, good people
Lazy Tiger Rag

To do the Lazy Tiger first you gotta move it slow
Never cross your feet, never let 'em leave the floor
Climb a ladder with your hands
At the top you slam the gate
while you shake your money-maker in a lazy
      figure eight

Lazy Tiger Rag, good people
Look at that tiger go

Stationary ride, don't forget to crack the whip
Make the Lazy Tiger pick it up a little bit
When you got him moving
crack again and make him rip
Here's what you have to do
if he gives you any lip

Step hard on his tail
Make a Lazy Tiger moan
Only thing he wanta do
is lay around at home
so kick him out of bed
Gotta teach him how to shag
Gotta hit him on the head
if you wanta make him rag
Chase him through the back door
out into the street
down around the corner
to a Lazy Tiger beat

Lazy Tiger Rag, good people
Lazy Tiger Rag
Lazy Tiger Rag, good people
Ride that tiger home

LEAVE THE LITTLE GIRL ALONE

She's wicked but she knows what she likes
She's wicked but she knows what she likes
Don't you underrate her
She's a navigator
She's wicked but she's such a delight

She lives in a world of her own
She lives in a world of her own
All the people there
know enough not to stare
They love her or they leave her alone

Leave the little girl alone
Won't you leave that poor girl alone?
To each and every one his own
I say leave that girl alone

She's twisted but she's got what it takes
She's twisted but she's got what it takes
She's got what it takes
to make her own mistakes
She's twisted but she's got what it takes

Leave the little girl alone
Won't you leave that poor girl alone?
To each and every one his own
I say leave that girl alone

Leave the little girl alone
Leave that little girl alone
She's keeping it tight
Gonna make out all right
Leave that little girl alone

She's vicious but she knows when to stop
She's vicious but she knows when to stop
She's makin' out fine
Knows where to toe the line
She's vicious but she knows when to stop

Leave the little girl alone
Won't you leave that poor girl alone?
To each and every one his own
I say leave that girl alone

_____

LET ME SING YOUR BLUES AWAY

Hop in the hack
Turn on the key
Pop in the clutch
Let the wheels roll free

Not a cloud in the sky
Such a sunny day
Push in the button
Let the Top Ten play

C'mon, honey, let me sing 'em away
C'mon, honey, let me sing 'em away
C'mon, honey, let me sing your blues away

Give me a little of that old-time love
I ain't never had near enough

Walk that walk
with style and grace
This ain't no knock-down
drag-out race

It don't matter much
Pick any gear
Grind you a pound and
drop the rear
Baby, baby, what can I say?
I'm here to drive your blues away

Sent a letter to a man I know
Said one for the money and two for the show
Waited all summer for his reply

Three to get ready and four to fly

Only two things in the world I love
That's rock and roll and my turtle-
    dove

When I was a younger man
I needed good luck
I'm a little bit older now
and I know my stuff

C'mon, honey, let me sing 'em away
C'mon, honey, let me sing 'em away
C'mon, honey, let me
sing your
blues
away

(Regrettably my only collaboration with the late Keith Godchaux)

_____

LIBERTY

Saw a bird with a tear in his eye
Walking to New Orleans—my, my, my
Hey, now, Bird, wouldn't you rather die
than walk this world when you're born
    to fly?

If I was the sun, I'd look for shade
If I was a bed, I would stay unmade
If I was a river I'd run uphill
And if you call me you know I will

Mmmm, freedom
Ooo, liberty
O . . . leave me alone
to find my own way home

I say what I mean and I don't give a damn
I do believe and I am who I am
Hey, now, Mama, come take my hand
Whole lotta shakin' all over this land

If I was an eagle I'd dress like a duck
Crawl like a lizard and honk like a truck
If I get a notion I'll climb this tree
or chop it down and you can't stop me

Mmmm, freedom
Ooo, liberty
O . . . leave me alone
to find my own way home

Went to the well but the water was dry
Dipped my bucket in the clear blue sky
Looked in the bottom and what did I see?
The whole damned world looking back
    at me

If I was a bottle I'd spill for love
Sake of mercy I'd kill for love
If I were a juicer I'd binge for love
If I were a coward I'd cringe for love

Freedom
Liberty
Leave me alone
to find my own way home

LITTLE FOXES

Sleepyhead
off to bed
The stars all twinkle bright
One by one
on the run
chase the moon tonight

In their den
snug and tight
the little foxes sleep
Bullfrog sing
Crickets ring
Midnight shadows creep

You can't see the little foxes
Running through the woods at night
You can't see the hand that guides
Trust that it will guide you right

Safe and sound
Ring around
the roses in your head
Nightlamp low
Time to go
Up the stairs to bed

The moon is shining
Through the lemon tree
Three blind mice in
har-mo-ny
Singing on the doorstep
way down under the breeze
"What about me?"

The cat is washing in the hall
The dog is by the fire
Since you cannot have it all
Pick your true desire

In their den
snug and tight
the little foxes sleep
Bullfrog sing
Crickets ring
Midnight shadows creep
Midnight shadows creep
Midnight shadows
Midnight shadows
Midnight shadows creep

LOOSE LUCY

Loose Lucy is my delight
She comes running and we ball all night
Round and round and round and round
Don't take much to get me on the ground

She's my yo-yo, I'm her string
Listen to the birds on the hotwire sing

Singing: Yeah, yeah, yeah, yeah
Singing: Thank you
for a real good time

I got jumped coming home last night
Shadow in the alley turned out all my lights
Round and round and round and round
Don't take much to lay me on the ground

Loose Lucy—was she sore!
Says I know you don't want my love no more

Singing: Yeah, yeah, yeah, yeah
Singing: Thank you
for a real good time

Be-bop baby, how can this be?
I know you been out a-cheating on me
Round and round and round and round
Don't take much to get the word around

Cross my heart and I hope to die
I was just hanging out with the other guys

Singing: Yeah, yeah, yeah, yeah
Singing: Thank you
for a real good time

Went back home with two black eyes
But you know I'll love her till the day I die
Round and round and round and round
Don't take much to get the word around

I like your smile but I ain't your type
Don't shake the tree when the fruit
    ain't ripe
Singing: Yeah, yeah, yeah, yeah
Singing:
Thank you
for a real good time

LOSER

If I had a gun for every ace I've drawn
I could arm a town the size of Abilene
Don't you push me, baby, 'cause I'm moaning low
You know I'm only in it for the gold

All that I am asking for is ten gold dollars
I could pay you back with one good hand
You can look around about the wide world over
You'll never find another honest man

Last fair deal in the country, sweet Suzy
Last fair deal in the town
Put your gold money where your love is, baby
Before you let my deal go down

Don't you push me, baby
because I'm moaning low
I know a little something
you won't ever know
Don't you touch hard liquor,
just a cup of cold coffee
Gonna get up
in the morning and go

Everybody's bragging and drinking that wine
I can tell the Queen of Diamonds by the way she shine
Come to Daddy on an inside straight
I got no chance of losing this time
No, I got no chance of losing this time

LOVE IN THE AFTERNOON

Love—Love in the afternoon
Outside the window
an organ grinder's tune

Rhythm, wine
A touch of Jamaica
Twilight time with a Kingston lady
All the time in the world
for me and that girl

Sweet—She sang sweetly
Come back soon
Come back for more of that love
in the afternoon

Breezes blow by me
in the afternoon
She sings sweetly
an organ grinder's tune

Finally recovered from last year's round
of *bye-bye baby blues*
All I crave today
Some love in the afternoon

Love—Love in the afternoon
It's easy as she goes
like an organ grinder's tune

Gone with the moon
any old trouble
can't leave too soon
Trouble's no part of what I want
especially in the afternoon
Singing

Sleeping till two
Waking to make more
love in the afternoon

Mama's on parole
Papa's in the pen
My baby got stuck
with five to ten

Oh, no
Lovin' spoonful
No more
Lovin' spoonful

Here's one for Peter
Here's one for Paul
Here's one for the lady
Who loves us all

See through sneakers
Cellophane sox
Tell she's a bitch
by the way she walks

Oh, no
Lovin' spoonful
No more
Lovin' spoonful

If dogs could crow
and hens could bark
wouldn't get no sleep
on Noah's Ark

Lovin' spoonful
gobble your core
Spit out the seeds
and ask for more

Oh, no
Lovin' spoonful
No more
Lovin' spoonful

Look in the mirror
and slap my face
Broken glass all
over the place

22–20
44–10
Won't get stuck
on you again

Oh, no
Lovin' spoonful
No more
Lovin' spoonful

MAD

I got born on Sunday, started work next day
I had to wait till Friday to get my first week's pay
I spent it all on Saturday, got drunk as I could be
Ended in the city jail for blood in first degree

That made me mad
Well, that made me mad
It made me so damned mad
it made me crazy

I run into Billy Bligh strolling through the town
I can't take the way he walks or how he lays it down
I said: Give me one good reason why you should be alive
You stepped on my shadow and now you've got to die

'Cause you made me mad
Well, that made me mad
It made me so damned mad
it made me crazy

Being in a mellow mood I went to see Marie
She was sitting on the swing with my good friend McGee
McGee said: Don't get hot and bent, it's plain for all to see
If it ain't twenty others, hell, it might as well be me

And that made me mad
Well, that made me mad
It made me so damned mad
it made me crazy

Devil come to get me long before my day
Said: "I need a man like you and I can raise your pay
Give you fifty-dollar bill and all the beer in town
'Cause you're a natural mother's son, as best as can be found"

The ladies call me Sugar but my name is Stainless Steel
They all know the way I look and love the way I feel
When I come to call on you, you better be in bed
'Cause if you're out a-hooking, remember what I said

That makes me mad
Well, that makes me mad
It makes me so damned mad
it makes me crazy

Take your flimflam boogeyman, turn him upside down
Stick his head right up his hat and drive him in the ground
The things he tries to tell you would make the Devil smile
One hand in your pocket and praying all the while

It makes me mad
Well, it makes me mad
It makes me so damned mad
it makes me crazy

MAN OF SOME DISTINCTION

In the springtime of my enemy
With winter at my heels
Across a printed borderline
The roving bandit steals
The peaches of the tree he took
And likewise stole the branch
He will snatch the trunk and root
If given half a chance
He will steal the seed as well
So none may grow again
Sell the plot on which it grew
If five can get him ten

You don't have to help him out
Knows how to help himself
While you stand by in innocence
And let him guard the wealth
Soon there'll be no wealth to guard
And he will drop away
Like any other parasite
What more can I say?
He masquerades as wisdom
His investments rarely fail
He props up the economy
And holds the keys to jail

He's a man of some distinction
And he takes no reprimand
Reach way down in your pocket
If you want to shake his hand

He drives the farmer from the land
The plowman from the field
Forecloses on the destitute
When crops refuse to yield

He draws the laws in such a way
An honest man must cheat
To lay upon the family board
The cheapest cut of meat
Desperate circumstances are
His butter, bread and wine
If they don't happen naturally
They happen by design

'This is how it's got to be'
Is all he has to say
He cares for your tomorrow
Even less than your today
He creeps among legalities
A termite in the walls
He's always safely out of sight
The day they finally fall
There's no kind of provision
To undo the harm he's done;
Halt the suicidal trigger
Of another desperate gun

He's a man of some distinction
And he takes no reprimand
Reach way down in your pocket
If you want to shake his hand

MASON'S CHILDREN

Mason died on Monday
We bricked him in the wall
All his children grew and grew
They never grew so tall before
They may never grow so tall again

We dug him up on Tuesday
He'd hardly aged a day
Taught us all we ever knew
We never knew so much before
We may never know so much again

Mason was a mighty man
A mighty man was he
All he said: When I'm dead and gone
don't you weep for me

The wall collapsed on Wednesday
We chalked it up to fate
All his children ran and hid
We never hid so well before
Swore we'd never show our face again

Thursday came and Friday
with fires tall and bright
Mason's children cooked the stew
and cleaned up when the feast was through
Swore we'd never had such times before

Take me to the Reaper Man
to pay back what was loaned
If he's in some other land
write it off as stoned

Mason was a mighty man
A mighty man was he
All he said: When I'm dead and gone
don't you weep for me

(An unrecorded GD song dealing obliquely with Altamont)

144

MAYBE SHE'S A BLUEBIRD

All of my fancy
All of my dreams come true
Just to be here with you
For the last dream

All of my life
Starts to make sense now
I think I see what it means

When I was a beggar
When I was a thief
When I was caught up
Was you that brought relief

Sometimes you amaze me
Sometimes make me crazy
Maybe you're a bluebird
That will never fly away

Not fly away, no
Not fly away
Maybe you're a bluebird
Who will never fly away

MEET ME IN MEXICO

Meet me in Mexico
I'm going way below
Meet me in Mexico
Way on down below

May go by aeroplane
Streetcar or streamline train
Limousine or walking cane
I'm going just the same

May go by riverboat
Taxicab or billy goat
Swim there in my overcoat
I'm going just the same

Meet me in Mexico
I'm going way below
Meet me in Mexico
Way on down below

May go by rollerskate
Diesel truck or Ford V-8
Mail me in a packing crate
I'm going just the same

Might go by rattlesnake
Naked in a birthday cake
'less I'm making some mistake
I'm going to Mexico

way on down
way on down
way on down . . . To Mexico

Might go there in a hearse
Second gear or in reverse
Crawl there on my face or worse
I'm going just the same

Might ride there on a breeze
Dogsled pulled by Pekingese
Walk my legs off to the knees
I'm going just the same

way on down
way on down
way on down . . . To Mexico

Meet me in Mexico
I'm going way below
Meet me in Mexico
Way on down below

MIDNIGHT GETAWAY

I heard you round about midnight
slipping out of the bed
You thought that I was fast asleep

Heard your slippers in the midnight hallway
and I heard you rustling around
trying not to make a sound

Heard the tap of your high heels
and the click of the lock on the door
Baby, I hope you know what you're doing

Heard you walking down the stairs
and I counted them one by one
One for each year that flew by

Heard you stop and turn back once
Then I thought I heard you sigh
Or maybe it was the breeze

Heard the jingle of your keys
Then you stumbled and cursed the cat
that was sleeping on the stairs under the stars

Heard you open the car door softly
You must have been there half an hour
turning it over round in your head

Were you sat there waiting
for me to come down and call your name?
I wonder, were you waiting for me?

Waiting for me . . .
Waiting for me . . .
Waiting for me?

Then I heard the motor turn over
and I heard you driving away
way before the break of day

Heard your engine for a long, long time
'cause the night was so cold and quiet
as you made your getaway in the night

MIDNIGHT TOWN

I guess you think
I'd never want to harm you
You better beware
That dream you dream
In time it could demand
the very ground on which I stand

Maybe you think
that I am just a stranger
or maybe recall
I knew your name
You wrote it on the wall
in letters black and tall

Way down
Way down
in Midnight Town

When midnight dawns
upon each painted martyr in the circus
maybe you'll recall
we met before
So, please, don't you accuse me
of dealing with you loosely

Way down
Way down
in Midnight Town

MIGHT AS WELL

Great North Special, were you on board?
You can't find a ride like that no more
Night the chariot swung down low
Ninety-nine children had a chance to go

One long party from front to end
Tune to the whistle going 'round the bend
No big hurry, what do you say?
Might as well travel the elegant way

Might as well, might as well
Might as well, might as well
Might as well, might as well
Might as well, might as well

Ragtime solid for twenty-five miles
then slip over to the Cajun style
Bar car loaded with rhythm and blues
Rock and roll wailing in the old caboose

Long train running from coast to coast
bringing 'long the party where they need
        it the most
Whup on the boxcar, beat on the bell
Nothing else shaking so you might just as
        well

Might as well, might as well
Might as well, might as well
Might as well, might as well
Might as well, might as well

Never had such a good time
        in my life before
I'd like to have it one time more
One good ride from start to end
I'd like to take that ride again
Again

Run out of track and I caught the plane
Back in the county with the blues again
Great North Special been on my mind
Might like to ride it just one more time

Might as well, might as well
Might as well, might as well
Might as well, might as well
Might as well, might as well

(In the early seventies a train was leased for a trip across Canada, stopping in major cities to throw music festivals. On board were Delaney and Bonny, Ian and Silvia, The Band, Janis Joplin, The Grateful Dead, Charlebois, the New Riders, and various other acts that boarded from time to time. Everyone agreed we had just about the best time of our collective lives in that week of nonstop music and partying. Nearing her last days, Janis, for one, wished aloud that the ride would never have to stop.)

MIRALDA

Wild stallion, black on white
I've got to trap and ride him
before my neighbor shoots on sight
to find out what's inside him

Blue-black blood and guts of steel
He does not know a master
The wind roars 'round the great divide
Marudio runs faster

I rode eight days to Saratoga
Gambled for a blue-eyed mare
Whose name was Sweet Miralda
Pale lank mane like a lady's hair

I bet my saddle, stock, and ranch
and all I had to spend
I watched the cards fall in a trance
Ace, king, jack, deuce, and ten

My high cards were diamonds
Jack of spades and deuces wild
My demon threw that jack away
I played it like a child

But with the luck a child may rule
Or some would say the lush
I broke that straight like a holy fool
and drew a royal flush

Oh, Miralda
Whoa—Oh
Miralda
I'll ride you home

I ride Miralda night and day
sleep by her silky side
until I come where my Rancho lay
sidesaddle on the great divide

With painted dust of Arizona
clinging to her hide,
Marudio, Cabrone
I've brought you a bride

I feed Miralda golden wheat
Brush her till she flashes
Tether her to a piñon tree
and hide out in the rashes

Dashing through the perfumed wind
I see Marudy falter
I've as good as saddled him
with bride, spur, and halter

Deliver me from girls and horses
I can't pick a winner
Miralda looked up only once
then went back to her dinner

Which reminds me of a girl
I loved once long ago
whose name was Esmeralda
from Ciudad Guerrero

Esmeralda could have tamed,
instead indifference served me
Broke my heart and caused me pain
She must have not deserved me

Be that as it may and might
this sad fact I won't alter
Marudio got broke that night
with no spur, whip, or halter

MISSION IN THE RAIN

I turn and walk away
then I come round again
It looks as though tomorrow
I'll do very much the same

I must turn down your offer
but I'd like to ask a break
You know I'm ready to give everything
for anything I take

Someone called my name
You know I turned around to see
It was midnight in the Mission
and the bells were not for me

Come again
Walking along in the Mission
in the rain
Come again
Walking along in the Mission
in the rain

Ten years ago I walked this street
my dreams were riding tall
Tonight I would be thankful
Lord for any dream at all

Some folks would be happy
just to have one dream come true
but everything you gather
is just more that you can lose

Come again
Walking along in the Mission
in the rain

Come again
Walking along in the Mission
in the rain

All the things I planned to do
I only did halfway
Tomorrow will be Sunday
born of rainy Saturday

There's some satisfaction
in the San Francisco rain
No matter what comes down
the Mission always looks the same

Come again
Walking along in the Mission
in the rain
Come again
Walking along in the Mission
in the rain

MISSISSIPPI HALF-STEP UPTOWN TOODLELOO

On the day that I was born
Daddy sat down and cried
I had the mark just as plain as day
which could not be denied
They say that Cain caught Abel
rolling loaded dice,
ace of spades behind his ear
and him not thinking twice

Half-step
Mississippi Uptown Toodleloo
Hello baby I'm gone, good-bye
Half a cup of rock and rye
Farewell to you, old Southern sky
I'm on my way—on my way

If all you got to live for
is what you left behind
get yourself a powder charge
and seal that silver mine
I lost my boots in transit, babe
A pile of smoking leather
Nailed a retread to my feet
        and prayed for better weather

Half-step
Mississippi Uptown Toodleloo
Hello baby I'm gone, good-bye
Half a cup of rock and rye
Farewell to you, old Southern sky
I'm on my way—on my way

They say that when your ship comes in
the first man takes the sails
The second takes the afterdeck
The third the planks and rails
What's the point to calling shots?
This cue ain't straight in line
Cueball's made of Styrofoam
and no one's got the time

Half-step
Mississippi Uptown Toodleloo
Hello baby I'm gone, good-bye
Half a cup of rock and rye
Farewell to you, old Southern sky
I'm on my way—on my way
Across the Rio Grand-eo
   Across the lazy river
   Across the Rio Grand-eo
   Across the lazy river

MISTER CHARLIE

I take a little powder
I take a little salt
I put it in my shotgun
and I go walking out

Chuba-chuba
Wooley-booley
Looking high
Looking low
Gonna scare you up and shoot you
'Cause Mister Charlie told me so

I won't take your life
Won't even take a limb
Just unload my shotgun
and take a little skin

Chuba-chuba
Wooley-booley
Looking high
Looking low
Gonna scare you up and shoot you
'Cause Mister Charlie told me so

Well, you take a silver dollar
Take a silver dime
Mix 'em both together
in some alligator wine

I can hear the drums
Voodoo all night long
Mister Charlie tellin' me
I can't do nothin' wrong

Chuba-chuba
Wooley-booley
Looking high
Looking low
Gonna scare you up and shoot you
'Cause Mister Charlie told me so

Now Mister Charlie told me
Thought you'd like to know
Give you a little warning
before I let you go

Chuba-chuba
Wooley-booley
Looking high
Looking low
Gonna scare you up and shoot you
'Cause Mister Charlie told me so

MOLLY DEE

Wish I was in Chattanooga
Paris, France, or Rome
Anyplace but California
Anywhere but home
Acapulco, Minnesota,
Cincinnati, Chad—
I don't care how good it is
Don't even care how bad

Bali Hi or Bali Low
or Bali in-between
Somewhere I've never been
Or hardly ever seen
Years go slipping by like weeks
I know that can't be right
My love life has me twisted
till I dream of it at night

Oh, Molly Dee—I'm setting you free
Give back the love you borrowed,
    whoa-oh

There's a limit to the limit
even love can bear
look to see how high the moon
it isn't even there . . .
nothing where a star provoked
a wish your heart proclaimed
All along the water tower
singing in the rain

Maybe I did something you
can never quite forgive
I'm sorry from the heart, you know
but I still have to live
No point at all to prove whose moves
have brought us where we are
We make it sound so serious
But that's just who we are

Oh, Molly Dee—I'm setting you free
Give back the love you borrowed,
    whoa-oh

Sunshine tangled in my hair,
a beam caught in my eye
Every now and then appears
a fool somewhat like I
Half-a-dollar moon arising
on my windowsill
If I were easily moved to tears
I think perhaps I'd spill

Half a year in solitary
staring at the wall
I know every chip and crack
and, baby, that ain't all
Jaybird on the windowsill
a catfight in the street
Hand me down my walking cane
and raise me to my feet

Oh, Molly Dee—I'm setting you free
Give back the love you borrowed,
    whoa-oh

Hangman, do your duty
tie a rope around my neck
Bought too much on credit
Can't begin to pay the check
I can't even come up with
the interest on the loan
I'd call to say I'm sorry
but I can't afford the phone

I woke up one morning
without any song to sing
If I can last through this
I can last through anything
It either comes too easy
or it doesn't come at all

You think you have a calling
It depends on who you call

Oh, Molly Dee—I'm setting you free
Give back the love you borrowed,
        whoa-oh

Looking back upon the years
to see where I went wrong
Not too much time for friendship
And too much time for song
When the music's over
The singing's said and done
Looking back is looking right
into a loaded gun

Oh, Molly Dee—I'm setting you free
Give back the love you borrowed,
        whoa-oh

Sing a song of seven cents
a pocket full of sand
A bird or two behind each bush
but nothing in the hand
Used to play with Eric Dolphy
Started out with Fats
I don't play much anymore
There ain't no call for sax

Something singing in the sky
but not like any bird
Longest, sweetest melancholy
note I ever heard
Pretty close to sundown
so it might have been a star
strumming the horizon like
the string of a guitar

Oh, Molly Dee—hold on and see
We'll roll along tomorrow—whoa-oh

Sometimes it's all right to wander
homeless in the street,
sacking out in open cars
and lining up to eat
Maybe I'll get lucky
one more time before I die
Cure our ills with dollar bills
I hate to see you cry

If they made a road map of
the backroads of the heart
we might find where we went wrong
and make another start
As it is we travel blind
trusting to a song
We may seek and never find
but still we roll along

Oh, Molly Dee—hold on and sing
A song for a long tomorrow

    —whoa-oh

(Written along with France: see notes for that song.*)

155

MOUNTAINS OF THE MOON

Cold mountain water
the jade merchant's daughter
Mountains of the Moon, Electra
Bow and bend to me
Hi-ho the Carrion Crow
Folderolderiddle
Hi-ho the Carrion Crow
Bow and bend to me

Hey, Tom Banjo
Hey, a laurel
More than laurel
You may sow
More than laurel
You may sow

Hey, the laurel
Hey, the city
In the rain
Hey, hey
Hey, the white wheat
Wavin' in the wind

Here is a feast of solitude★
A fiddler grim and tall
Plays to dancing kings and wives
Assembled in the hall
Of lost, long, lonely times
Fairy Sybil flying
All along the all along the
Mountains of the Moon

Hey, Tom Banjo
It's time to matter
The Earth will see you
on through this time
The Earth will see you on
through this time

Down by the water
The Marsh King's Daughter
Did you know?
Clothed in tatters
Always will be
Tom, where did you go?

Mountains of the Moon, Electra
Mountains of the Moon
All along the
All along the
Mountains of the Moon

Hi-ho the Carrion Crow
Folderolderiddle
Hi-ho the Carrion Crow
Bow and bend to me
Bend to me

★The lines to this verse as originally recorded are:
Twenty degrees of solitude/Twenty degrees in all/All the dancing kings and
wives/assembled in the hall/lost is a long and lonely time/Fairy Sybil flying/All
along the/All along the/Mountains of the Moon

MUST BE THE MOON

I hear singing high and thin
like a woman in the wind
Wailing music with no tune
No one there—must be the moon

Fact of the matter
I never knew you
Only some picture
My fantasy drew
Portrait in yellow
Shadows in blue
Might have been sweet
But it never was true
Never was true—it never was true

If I could dream this dream anew
From the start to the end with you
Knowing what a dream can do
I believe we could make it through
Make it on through—make it on through

You came from Picasso's pink
    and blue days
A harlequin figure with American ways
Silent as bricks on a back-street wall
Deep in my heart I can hear you call

I hear singing high and sweet
out my window in the street
Wailing music with no tune
No one there—must be the moon

Made up a love song
I sang it to you
It came from the heart
So it might have been true

Not that it mattered
you smiled through a tear
packed up your suitcase
and left me right here
Left me right here/left me right here

If I could dream this dream anew
From the start to the end with you
Knowing what a dream can do
I believe we could make it through
Make it on through
Make it on through

I hear singing high and thin
like a woman in the wind
Wailing music with no tune
No one there
Must be the moon

You were as good as
It takes to believe
You knew how to give
I just couldn't receive
I've kicked around now
Like some people must
to learn what to value
and finally to trust

If I could dream this dream anew
From the start to the end with you
Knowing what a dream can do
I believe we could make it through
Make it on through
Make it on through

NEW SPEEDWAY BOOGIE

Please don't dominate the rap, Jack
if you got nothing new to say
If you please, don't back up the track
This train got to run today

Spent a little time on the mountain
Spent a little time on the hill
Heard some say: *Better run away*
Others say: *You better stand still*

Now I don't know but I been told
it's hard to run with the weight of gold
Other hand I heard it said
it's just as hard with the weight of lead

Who can deny? Who can deny?
It's not just a change in style
One step done and another begun
in I wonder how many miles?

Spent a little time on the mountain
Spent a little time on the hill
Things went down we don't understand
but I think in time we will

Now I don't know but I been told
in the heat of the sun a man died of cold
Do we keep on coming or stand and wait
with the sun so dark and the hour so late?

You can't overlook the lack, Jack
of any other highway to ride
It's got no signs or dividing lines
and very few rules to guide

Spent a little time on the mountain
Spent a little time on the hill
I saw things getting out of hand
I guess they always will

I don't know but I been told
if the horse don't pull you got to carry
    the load
I don't know whose back's that strong
Maybe find out before too long

One way or another
One way or another
One way or another
this darkness got to give
One way or another
One way or another
One way or another
this darkness got to give

(Written as a reply to an indictment of the Altamont affair by pioneer rock critic Ralph J. Gleason)

NO PLACE HERE

Ashes, Ashes, all fall down
Judy run naked all round the town
I know something you don't know
But I'm gonna tell you now

Good-bye, baby, the train don't leave
    from here
Hello, Mama, the grass ain't greener
On the far, far side of a Tampa evening
No place here to rest your head,
    you better go

Rain gonna fall, wind gonna blow
Didn't we do it, didn't we, though?
Babe, if you won't stoke my flame
Don't come jerk me round again

We did that walk in single file
More or less in the best of style
Ashes, babe, we all fell down
But didn't we know we would?

Good-bye, baby, the train don't leave
    from here
Hello, Mama, the grass ain't greener
On the far, far side of a Tampa evening
No place here to rest your head,
    you better go

Dancing barefoot in the street
But not for want of sock or shoe
It rained all night and rained all day
But there's not a drop on you

Rained all night and it rained all day
Rain come floated your house away
I know you know I know, too
It don't matter to me or you

Good-bye, baby, the train don't leave
    from here
Hello, Mama, the grass ain't greener
On the far, far side of a Tampa evening
No place here to rest your weary head,
    you better go

Rain gonna fall, wind gonna blow
Didn't we do it, didn't we, though?
All you gotta do, play fair and tough and
You get what you want if you want it
    enough

(I think this lyric from early 1970 manages to retain its own personality despite having undergone a dramatic cannibalization of its phrases into more than half a dozen other lyrics, including: "That Train Don't Run Here Anymore," "Bertha," "Crooked Judge," "Loser," "Kick It On Down," "Truckin'," and "Ramble on Rose.")

NORTHEAST BY WEST

Twenty-three miles northeast by west
a bad attack of murder
seemed to break out everywhere
there was no known cure

Really tried to warn the crowd
Just try to stay away
but people felt they had a right
and showed up anyway

Northeast by west I ride
At angles to all borders
I'm not taking any side
Or giving any orders

I had my insides hanging out
from dangling round all summer
Demanding that we twist and shout
Or kick the damn thing under

I may need a whole new part
or just a dab of paint
Chickenshit can be an art
I guess, unless it ain't

Northeast by west I ride
By no man's lawful orders
Southwest by east I ride
At angles to all borders

Here kitty, kitty, come lap it up
You'd best beware that stuff
It's got blood and guts and you'll
just have to throw it up

You might disagree with me
It's your right to be wrong
Anyway, I got my say
even if it's just a song

Northeast by west I ride
At angles to all borders
I'm not taking any side
And no one gives me orders

Is it late enough to say
Good morning everyone?
Or is that just an arc light glare
disguised as a rising sun?

Say you saw me passing through
and that I was a friend
If it had not of been for you
God knows how it would end

_____

ONE THING TO TRY

Break out your bottle, be in trouble by noon
Never get satisfaction 'cause you boil too soon
Them downtown chippies know your weight to the ounce
but the harder you fall, Jack, the higher you bounce

Stoke up your gator, be ready to ride
but keep your hands and your heart inside
Take it as far as you wanta go
till we can't see the desert for the burning snow

but if you're in a hurry
and really got to go . . .
If you're in a hurry
might have to find out slow
that it's one thing to try
and another to fly
You get there quicker
just a step at a time
It's one thing to bark
another to bite
The show ain't over
till you pack up at night

Out of ninety-nine people all running around
Not one in a hundred got his feet on the ground
You find one in a thousand holding some in reserve
for when the real true action come around the curve
Take care of your people, get some of them fed
Hide the ones in trouble out under your bed
Keep an eye to the future, an ear to the past
After thinking it over, notice nothing much lasts

If you're in a hurry
and really got to go . . .
If you're in a hurry
might have to find out slow
that it's one thing to try
and another to fly
You get there quicker

just a step at a time
It's one thing to bark
another to bite
The show ain't over
till you pack up at night

Don't ever let it get the best of you
Plan what you can and let the rest shine through
Just so many angles you can possibly see
Figure on those, let the other ones be
Don't be out collecting more than you need
Got a lot of things growing but keep watching those seeds
Got to share in December what you planted in May
If the harvest is empty find some other good way

but if you're in a hurry
and really got to go . . .
If you're in a hurry
might have to find out slow
that it's one thing to try
and another to fly
You get their quicker
just a step at a time
It's one thing to bark
another to bite
The show ain't over
till you pack up at night

ONLY THE STRANGE REMAIN

Been searching in sectors private and dark
With the eye of a witness—silent and stark
Seen everything that goes on in the night
Things that are twisted and hid from the light
Where Only the Strange remain

I pack my sack with a fistful of fire
There are cut-throats and thieves in this night of desire
Who steals my treasure must contend with its flame
Where only the strange remain
Where Only the Strange remain

Looking deep and then deeper into every face
Past beauty and wisdom, past gender and race
I see a lone hungry wolf in a shining blue flame
And only the strange remain
Only the Strange remain

If truth is impossible, so is the lie
Theres no in-between, you can't swim, you can't fly
At the uttermost link at the end of our chain
Only the Strange Remain
Only the Strange Remain

Wolves of the winterland, teeth broken white
Sons of the harvest and daughters of night
Dancing in thunder to conquer the rain
Where only the strange remain
Only the Strange Remain

Tell me, friend, have you noticed of late how
Only the strange remain?
I'm speaking about the cream of the strange
Not the merely weird, the far out of sight, or insane
No, only the strange remain
No, only the strange remain
No, no, only the strange remain

ONLY TO BELIEVE

I got a wartorn stripper
Keeps her price list in a loving cup
I got a wartorn stripper
Keeps her price list in a loving cup
I get so low at times
it's only to believe that I don't give it up

I look in all those faces
I hear words but no reply
I look in all those faces
I hear words but no reply
You want to be my baby?
You must be crazy, ain't no lie

Only to believe
It's only to believe
Only to believe and not
for any other reason I can see

I got consolidated rebop
Plush-lined veranda and a velvet cane
I got consolidated rebop
Laid out flat and
I call your name
If you had a lick of sense
you'd send me back directly where I came

Only to believe
It's only to believe
Only to believe and not
for any other reason I can see

OVER THE HILLS

That's not the sound of your regular number
I know that sound like I know my own name
Say, Mr. Matches, that's a pretty nice tune
I wonder if you'd play that tune again?

It went: Over the Hills and Far Away
a guitar player at the break of day
Playing Oh My Lady and Oh My Soul
Playing Whoa-oh and Over She Go
and I don't want to lose that feeling
I don't want to lose that feeling
I don't want that feeling to go—no

That's not the sound of your regular drummer
One drive to the nail and four to the bar
I know that beat like I know my own heart
What were you thinking when you played that part?

It went: Over the Hills and Far Away
a drummer drummin' at the break of day
Playing Oh My Lady and Oh My Soul
Playing Whoa-oh and Over She Go
and I don't want the feeling to go—no
No, I don't want that feeling to go

That's not the voice of your regular singer
Been hearing that song since I was born
When I was a baby rocked in my cradle
Bright and early in the frosty morning

It gives me pleasure, it gives me peace
Gives me something to remember when seasons fly by
I can't recall the words or the tune so clearly
but I know when I hear it and I love it dearly

That's not the sound of your regular number
I know that sound like I know my own name
Say, Mr. Matches, that's a pretty nice tune
I wonder if you'd play that tune again?

_____

PALM SUNDAY

The river so white
The mountain so red
and with the sunshine
over my head
The honky-tonks are
all closed and hushed
It must be
Palm Sunday
again

The sky is so green
Clouds of canary
Blood moon rise like
a fat ripe cherry
Sunset quiet as
a benediction
One true love,
the rest is fiction

If I stay longer
trouble will find me
An epitaph and a
sheet to wind me
A passable day
for the least of men
it must be
Palm Sunday
again

(Verse one appears on the Garcia recording; two and three were written subsequently.)

PARCEL OF DOOM

You had a house with forty-nine rooms
A cellar of wine and a parcel of doom
A gate at the door with a chain and a lock
A book of the hours and a grandmother clock
You had nearly everything you could desire
a lover, a lantern, a bath, and a fire
You tried to shake the hand in your sleeve
But the more you see the less you believe

Joanne . . . whoo-whoo, Joanne

Let's get away from here, Joanne
It's just another bird in the hand
A fourteen-karat place to die
You don't like it—neither do I

You fought for the right to be wretched as sin
To carve the Lord's Prayer on the head of a pin
To answer all questions with: *What does it prove?*
To pass up your chance without making your move
you fought for the right to be misunderstood
To squander your talent and come to no good
To be mentally crazy, retarded and sick
Your wounds are your own, no one else's to lick

Joanne . . . whoo-whoo, Joanne

With all of these things that welled up inside
What's left of your conscience crumpled and died
Inviting us in with a wave of your hand
We raided your kitchen—me and Joanne

We licked your plates, looked over your home
Took a sheet of your tissue to play on your comb
A tune that was popular long ago
I remember it well—the name I *don't* know

I snatched up your parcel of doom from Joanne
Who attempted to leave it behind in a can
I said: *Are you crazy? Without this we're lost*
She stammered and stuttered: *But look at the cost*

Joanne . . . whoo-whoo, Joanne

There's one thing I cling to, intending to keep
The rest is like music you hear in your sleep
A parcel of doom is worth two in the clutch
Or ten in the future, which isn't worth much
As for the present, this point that exists,
Just guess at the reason I'm telling you this
I fought for the right to have nothing to say
Now me and Joanne must be on our way

Joanne . . . whoo-whoo, Joanne

PIECES OF EIGHT

All the old winds wail again
It's good to feel them as I run
      to save my skin
Cut the chain link, jump the ditches
Heighdy Ho, you sons-of-bitches
It's crying time on the federal ten
A man escaped from the Georgia pen

Pieces of eight haunt my dreams
Pieces of eight lying low, lying low
Low, low let it lie . . . lie low
Hook up with a couple of friends
split up the loot and do it again

The will to be free melts prison bars
      away
with a little ingenuity and a willingness
      to pay
Compromise the cellblock watch
Then you buy the guards
It helps if you can learn to deal
a wicked pack of cards

Pieces of eight haunt my dreams
Pieces of eight lying low, lying low
Wake, sleep, eat revenge
I won't wait for parole
Been waking up in a shaking sweat
my blood running cold

Change for two bits—three nickels and
      a dime
For you they called it politics, for me it
      was a crime
When it came to showdown time
You took yours and I got mine
Fifteen years on a federal rap
While you got off with a token slap

Pieces of eight haunt my dreams
Pieces of eight lying low, lying low
Dancing dead men grab my feet
Flashing teeth of gold
Wake me from a dream of hate
To run on through the cold

Cold shakes of dawn, South Bend bound
Half on bluff and half on luck I throw
      my weight around
I'll lie low and hide on out
with Angel Bright, whom I don't doubt
will put me up for a week or two
If she knows I'm looking for a crack at you

Pieces of eight haunt my dreams
Pieces of eight lying low, lying low
Cut the chain link, jump the ditches
Heighdy Ho, you sons-of-bitches
It's crying time on the federal ten
A man escaped from the Georgia pen

PLAYING IN THE BAND

Some folks trust to reason
Others trust to might
I don't trust to nothing
But I know it come out right

Say it once again now
Oh, I hope you understand
When it's done and over
Lord, a man is just a man

Playing
Playing in the band
Daybreak
Daybreak on the land

Some folks look for answers
Others look for fights
Some folks up in treetops
Just look to see the sights

I can tell your future
Look what's in your hand
But I can't stop for nothing
I'm just playing in the band

Playing
Playing in the band
Daybreak
Daybreak on the land

Standing on a tower
World at my command
You just keep a-turning
While I'm playing in the band

If a man among you
Got no sin upon his hand
Let him cast a stone at me
For playing in the band

Playing
Playing in the band
Daybreak
Daybreak on the land
Playing
Playing in the band
Daybreak
Daybreak on the land

PRODIGAL TOWN

Some are awaiting and some overtaking
the train—it's the last out of town
Wasn't much of a town anyway and I never
met anyone tempted to stay
To give it its due
It was where I met you
and you were my reason to stay
around
in a Prodigal Town

The seasonal change you can tell by the rain
Though the leaves never flame, it is Fall
I hear Vivaldi come drifting on by
from a ladies' quartet down the hall
If Heaven has sent it or
Hell has just lent it
I'm hardly the one to decide
this train that I ride
out of Prodigal Town

PROMONTORY RIDER

Promontory Rider
what makes you ride so high?
To put a loving star
back in an empty sky
Once the wind was warm and sweet,
the ladies in lace
But up there on the prominence
the tears just freeze your face
Promontory Rider—Territory Ranger . . . Step up

Found a stack of blank pictures
A passport out of Hell
Left here by a stranger
Seemed to wish me well
Signed Promontory Rider
Territory Ranger
Asking: Can you thread a needle?
Can you shoot the moon?
Walk the silver screen
to your judgment at High Noon
like any Promontory Rider? Territory Ranger . . . Step up

Ride on, ride on, ride on, ride

Ride upon the high ground,
ride upon the low
Promontory Rider
what makes you ride so slow?
Fit me out with heart and wings
and fill my head with crowns
I been crawling up this hill
but now I'm rolling down
Promontory Rider—Territory Ranger . . . Step up

Promontory Rider
you used to ride so high
I don't know these days
just seem to ride on by

Once the wind was warm and sweet
but this must be your taste
You don't change this chilly range
for any other place
Promontory Rider—Territory Ranger
Ride on, ride on . . . Step up

Moving on the high ground, moving on the low ground
Promontory Rider stepping so high now . . . Step up!

Promontory Rider
what made you ride so high?
To pluck a loving star
from out an empty sky
But Promontory Rider
that was many years ago
Movin' on the high ground,
movin' on the low

Promontory Rider, ride on, ride on
Territory Ranger, ride on, ride
Step right up and put that loving star
right back inside that empty sky
Promontory Rider, ride on, ride on
Territory Ranger . . . Step up

RAMBLE ON ROSE

Just like Jack the Ripper
Just like Mojo Hand
Just like Billy Sunday
In a shotgun ragtime band
Just like New York City
Just like Jericho
Pace the halls and climb the walls
Get out when they blow

Did you say your name was
Ramblin' Rose?
Ramble on, baby
Settle down easy
   Ramble on, Rose

Just like Jack and Jill
Mama told the sailor
One heat up and one cool down
Leave nothing for the tailor
Just like Jack and Jill
My Papa told the jailer
One go up and one come down
Do yourself a favor

Did you say your name was
Ramblin' Rose?
Ramble on, baby
Settle down easy
   Ramble on, Rose

I'm gonna sing you a hundred verses in ragtime
I know this song it ain't never gonna end
I'm gonna march you up and down the local county line
Take you to the leader of the band

Just like Crazy Otto
Just like Wolfman Jack
Sitting plush with a royal flush
Aces back to back

Just like Mary Shelley
Just like Frankenstein
Clank your chains and count your change
Try to walk the line

Did you say your name was
Ramblin' Rose?
Ramble on, baby
Settle down easy
   Ramble on, Rose

Good-bye, Mama and Papa
Good-bye, Jack and Jill
The grass ain't greener, the wine ain't sweeter
either side of the hill

Did you say your name was
Ramblin' Rose?
Ramble on, baby
Settle down easy
   Ramble on, Rose

RED CAR

Red car parked in the sunset
For Sale sign on the door
If I could afford that baby
I wouldn't have to walk no more
      —no more!

Red car, gleam in the sunset
You're my fate if I'm not wrong
If you run as fine as you look
Where could we not be by dawn?

Red car take me away
Way away to a better day
Wouldn't take more than a set of keys
To set my heart and my mind at ease

Nothing to show for the years
But a kind of a lukewarm blues
Now you come shining through my tears
How can I refuse?

Red car parked in the sunset
Gleaming with a touch of gold
You and me could go somewhere
It's foretold . . . Foretold!

Red car take me away
Way away to a better day
Wouldn't take more than a set of keys
To set my heart and my mind at ease

Warm as flesh to my caress
You almost seem to live
Whatever it takes to get you
That's what I'm gonna give

Red car parked in the sunset
Drive you in my dreams tonight
If you run as fine as you look

God knows you must run all right. . .
All right? All Right!

Red car take me away
Way away to a better day
Wouldn't take more than a set of keys
To set my heart . . . my heart . . .
      and my mind . . . at ease

Red car parked in the sunset
Gleaming with a touch of gold
You and me could go somewhere
It's foretold. . . .

Red car take me away
Take me to another day
Wouldn't take more than a set of keys
To set my heart . . . my heart. . .
      and my mind . . . at ease
Take me away—away—away

Red car, gleam in the sunset
You're my fate if I'm not wrong
If you run as fine as you look
Where could we not be by dawn?

Red car take me away
Way away to a better day
Wouldn't take more than a set of keys
To set my heart and my mind at ease . . .
      Ah please!

REELIN' AND A-PITCHIN'

Put down that bloody bottle
You're Noah's second son
See the water rising
well, you know you better run
Pick your lucky number
divide it how you may
Don't hang on no tighter
'cause you're only in the way . . .
    oooh, reelin'

reelin' and a-pitchin', uh-huh
Hot foot! Steppin' like the big boys do

Rock salt for the coffee
Pepper for the tea
Fist come through the window,
it hold a note which read:
I'm on pins and needles
cut with beer and gin
Open up the window
let the jelly roll right in . . .
    oooh, reelin'

reelin' and a-pitchin', uh-huh
Hot foot! Steppin' like the big boys do

Pickin' for my supper
Get it while it's hot
Raveled socks and mustard, baby
much worse in the pot
Order in the court
the judge is eatin' beans
Clerk is in the bathtub
sinkin' submarines . . .
    oooh, reelin'

reelin' and a-pitchin', uh-huh
Hot foot! Steppin' like the big boys do

Every inch the top cat
Says he been a rover
Got it here in detail
but you know he ain't no lover
Come on up and see me
Tell me what you mean
Woulda wrote a letter
but it might of made a scene . . .
    oooh, reelin'

reelin' and a-pitchin', uh-huh
Hot foot! Steppin' like the big boys do

High-heel Pumas
get a look at those knees
She does the funky chicken
but she's all right with me
Things be gettin' better
if they ain't gettin' worse
Give a little loving, whoa
Slam it in reverse . . . oooh, reelin'

reelin' and a-pitchin', uh-huh
Hot foot! Steppin' like the big boys do

RENO ROLL

There ain't nothing your Lord Almighty
your goddamned bloodstained dollar can buy around here

Reno roll
Higher, higher, higher
Reno roll
High, high . . .
Higher, higher, higher
Hey, Reno roll
It's unbelievable
How much you try
High, high,
Higher, higher, higher
Reno roll

I recall you knocking on the door one day
Believing my pretty girl's man was away
Now goddamn Reno, who you think I am
Walk in here, try to shake my hand?

Hey, Reno roll
Higher, higher, higher
Hey, Reno roll

You got nothing to complain about
But you do roll in when you should roll out

Reno roll
Higher, higher, higher
Reno roll
High, high . . .
Higher, higher, higher
Hey, Reno roll
It's unbelievable
How much you try
High, high,
Higher, higher, higher
Reno roll

Your dog run wild and your cat gone stray
Your horse been feeding on another man's hay
Shit out of luck but your folks are rich
So *goddamn Reno*, what the hell's your bitch?

Hey, Reno roll
Higher, higher, higher
Hey, Reno roll

Hot Choritta with a twist of red
Now damn-it-all, Reno, what the hell I said
Don't come waving those big fat bucks
You might be loaded but your style still sucks

Reno roll
Higher, higher, higher
Reno roll
High, high . . .
Higher, higher, higher
Hey, Reno roll
It's unbelievable
How much you try
High, high,
Higher, higher, higher
Reno roll

RESURRECTION RAG

In ruby light of a crescent moon
calm in the aftermath of doom
vines twine round
the slice of a knife . . .
flowers . . . seeds . . .
traces of life . . .

A wind from the west
plays flute on the holes
of ash blue craters,
melody rolls . . .
The voice of the song
so strangely like you
when the moon was white
and the sky was still blue

Resurrection Rag
The voice of the moon
I've heard it before
I remember the tune

Twelve crimson stars
shining bright overhead
They shall make music
to wake the dead

With breath in our bodies
we sing the refrain
With flesh on our bones
we feel softness and pain

With hope in our hearts
With trust in our eyes
We arise—We have risen
We arise—We have risen
We arise

(Written for the soundtrack of *Armageddon Rag*, which was never filmed. Merl Saunders performed this piece on the 1988 recording *Dinosaurs*. It is the second half of a composition titled Armageddon/Resurrection Rag.)

REUBEN AND CÉRISE

Cérise was brushing her long hair gently down
It was the afternoon of Carnival
as she brushes it gently down

Reuben was strumming the painted mandolin
It was inlaid with a pretty face in jade
Played the Carnival Parade

Cérise was dressing as Pirouette in white
when a fatal vision gripped her tight
Cérise, beware tonight

Reuben, Reuben, tell me truly true
I feel afraid and I don't know why I do
Is there another girl for you?

If you could see in my heart
you would know it's true
there is none, Cérise, except for you—
except for you
I swear to it on my very soul
If I lie may I fall down cold

When Reuben played the painted mandolin
the breeze would stop to listen in
before going its way again

Masquerade began when nightfall finally woke
Like waves against the bandstand dancers broke
to the painted mandolin

Looking out on the crowd, who is standing there?
Sweet Ruby Claire at Reuben stared
At Reuben stared
She was dressed as Pirouette in red
and her hair hung gently down

The crowd pressed 'round
Ruby stood as though alone
Reuben's song took on a different tone
and he played it just for her

The song he played was the Carnival Parade
Each note cut a thread of Cérise's fate
It cut through like a blade

Reuben was playing the painted mandolin
When Ruby froze and turned to stone
for the strings played all alone

The voice of Cérise from the face of the
        mandolin
singing: Reuben, Reuben, tell me true
for I have no one but you

*If you could see in my heart
you would know it's true
There is none, Cérise, except for you—
except for you*★

Reuben, swear to it on your very soul
If you lie I must fall down cold

Ahoy! Old Ferryman
Riverboat of Charon ride
Though alive, take Reuben to the other side
For his sweet Cérise has died

It's a long lonely walk from Hell
to the burying ground
Cérise may return
but don't you look around
for your glance would cut her down

★From this point the original Garcia version differs from the expanded version recorded on "Jack O' Roses." Page 182 gives the concluding verses as originally sung and recorded as *Rubin and Cherise*.

The truth of love an unsung song must tell
The course of love must follow blind
but Reuben looked behind

Reuben walked the streets of New Orleans till dawn
with the ghost of Cérise in his empty arms
and her hair hung gently down

RUBIN AND CHERISE—ORIGINAL CONCLUDING VERSES

The voice of Cherise
from the face of the mandolin
singing: Rubin, Rubin, tell me true
for I have no one but you

If you could see my heart
you would know it's true
There is none, Cherise, except for you—
        except for you
I swear to it on my very soul
If I lie, may I fall down cold

The truth of love
an unsung song must tell
The course of love must follow blind
without a look behind
Rubin walked through the streets
of New Orleans till dawn,
Cherise so lightly in his arms
and her hair hung gently down

RHAPSODY IN RED

I love to hear that Rhapsody in Red
It just knocks me right out of my head
Lifts me up here
just floatin' around
Sends me way up
and it don't let me down

I love to hear that Rhapsody in Red
on my feet or laid back in my bed
Takes me way back
where I don't mind
Takes me way back
in my time
my time

Sail away on that Rhapsody in Red
Don't care where those
other rainbows led
With all those northern lights
just blowing away
got no thought to relate
in the same old way
anyway

Love to feel it flood down to my soul
Loving feel just like in days of old
I sing blues
Where has it led?
Gimme some more
Rhapsody in Red
In Red

RIPPLE

If my words did glow
with the gold of sunshine
and my tunes were played
on the harp unstrung
would you hear my voice
come through the music
would you hold it near
as it were your own?

It's a hand-me-down
The thoughts are broken
Perhaps they're better
left unsung
I don't know
Don't really care
Let there be songs
to fill the air

Ripple in still water
when there is no pebble tossed
nor wind to blow

Reach out your hand
if your cup be empty
If your cup is full
may it be again
Let it be known
there is a fountain
that was not made
by the hands of men

There is a road
no simple highway
between the dawn
and the dark of night

And if you go
no one may follow
That path is for
your steps alone

Ripple in still water
when there is no pebble tossed
nor wind to blow

You who choose
to lead must follow
but if you fall
you fall alone
If you should stand
then who's to guide you?
If I knew the way
I would take you home

ROADHOG

I'm a straight-eight driver, I'm a neon wire
Gotta make a fire, I'm a roadhog
Got good bait, I'm a half-hour late
Gotta make a date with a dead dog
I'm a roadhog
yeah . . .
I'm a roadhog

Gonna tell you somethin' when my thyroid's pumpin'
Well, my heart gets jumpin' like a bullfrog
Just pulled out of a drive-in movie
I'm wound up tight and I'm feelin' groovy
Rock on over and cruise the strip
Drink a few beers, have a good ol' trip
I'm a roadhog
yeah . . .
I'm a roadhog

I'm a prostrate batter
I'm a number-five hatter
I'm a smooth-line chatter
I'm a roadhog
I'm an up-and-comer
I'm a flat-out bummer
I'm a toll-gate jumper
I'm a roadhog
yeah . . .
I'm a roadhog

I got four bald tires and a few crossed wires
Don't take no buyers, I'm a roadhog

(Ted Clare's croaking voice claimed lead honors on this tune, the signature song of the band Roadhog, which also included Rodney Albin, Jeffrey Dambrau, Shelley Ralston, Bill Summers, Jim MacPherson, and myself—three nights a week at the Green Earth Café on Market Street.)

I'm a high-rise tenant with a baseball pennant
Got a man in the Senate, I'm a roadhog
Yeah, yeah
I'm a roadhog
Roadhog!

ROCK COLUMBIA

Up on the mountain
feeling tired and alone
Thinking it over
over and over
I feel like a rock among stone
Even the sweet go wrong
Life is a heartbeat long
The urge to sing was strong
I swung my battered guitar like a net
and caught me a startled song—on the wing

Rock Columbia, Roll Columbia
Hey, good-lookin', you can make a poor boy sing
Rock the sun up, Roll the clouds away . . .
Columbia roll

Up on the mountain I saw
cities spread out like a map
San Francisco away to my left
New York right in my lap
I could see Boston below
Cincinnati, O-hi-o
People I love and know
frightened and fighting
portraits in lightning
It was a hell of a show
and I know

Rock Columbia, Roll Columbia
Hey, good-lookin', you can make a poor boy sing
Rock the sun up, Roll the clouds away . . .
Columbia roll

Portraits in lightning
Pretenses fell
Rock, bone, blood, and the bell
The roar of the wind
The faces within

Asking: *For who does it toll?*
It tolls for thee!

Rock Columbia, Roll Columbia
Hey, good-lookin', you can make a poor boy sing
Rock the sun up, Roll the clouds away . . .
Columbia roll

Darkness descended, I had
nothing to keep out the cold
I stumbled and fell a number of times
on the high shortcut to the road
Sweet road take me home
Rock, blood, and bone
I found my car
Though I was alone
I said: Driver, take me home
if you can

Rock Columbia, Roll Columbia
Hey, good-lookin', you can make a poor boy sing
Rock the sun up, Roll the clouds away . . .
Columbia roll

ROSEMARY

Boots were of leather
A breath of cologne
Her mirror was a window
She sat quite alone

All around her
the garden grew
scarlet and purple
and crimson and blue

She came and she went
and at last went away
The garden was sealed
when the flowers decayed

On the wall of the garden
a legend did say:
No one may come here
since no one may stay

ROSE OF SHARON

What you gonna call that pretty baby?
You must call it one thing or another
This one parted water,
    that one walked upon
Perhaps I'll call this child
    a Rose of Sharon

What's to be the ground that child
    walks upon?
Will it be solid rock or shifting sand?
Think I'll set him down on concrete highways
Think I'll bring him up to walk the land

I think I'll call him just another stranger
Believe I'll call him knocking
    at your door
Asking you for shelter from
    the lightning
Space to rest upon your kitchen floor

Will he be a man of constant sorrow?
Born to beg a coat against the storm?
Or will he want a house with many pillars?
And fire of a night to keep him warm?

And if a stranger comes for troubled shelter
With hounds and torchlight on his
    midnight trail
Will he find a moment free of madness there?
And ears that still can hear to tell his tale?

Then you could call that child the Rock
    of Ages
You could call him raft upon the flood
He has been the face of many races
He has been the palace in the blood

If that child should end up in a prison
As sometimes chance will deal to honest men
One room is like another to a stranger
Any man of worth will be his friend

Now what you gonna call that pretty baby?
You must call it one thing or another
Think I'll call him flame out on the water
Think I'll call him shore between the seas

Drop him on the rocks and he will shatter
Cut him with a blade and he will bleed
Plant him in the ground, he will rise up again
Sometimes as a flower, sometimes a reed

What you gonna call that pretty baby?
You must call him one thing or another
This one parted water, that one walked upon
Perhaps I'll call this child a Rose of Sharon

ROW, JIMMY

Julie catch a rabbit by his hair
Come back step, like to walk on air
Get back home where you belong
and don't you run off no more

Don't hang your head let the two-time roll
Grass shack nailed to a pinewood floor
Ask the time? Baby, I don't know
Come back later, we'll let it show

And I say row, Jimmy, row
Gonna get there?
I don't know
Seems a common way to go
Get down, row, row, row
row, row

Here's my half a dollar if you dare
double-twist when you hit the air
Look at Julie down below
the levee doin' the do-pas-o

And I say row, Jimmy, row
Gonna get there?
I don't know
Seems a common way to go
Get down, row, row, row
row, row

Broken heart don't feel so bad
Ain't got half o' what you thought you had
Rock your baby to and fro
Not too fast and not too slow

And I say row, Jimmy, row
Gonna get there?
I don't know
Seems a common way to go
Get down, row, row, row
row, row

That's the way it's been in town
ever since they tore the jukebox down
Two-bit piece don't buy no more
not so much as it done before

And I say row, Jimmy, row
Gonna get there?
I don't know
Seems a common way to go
Get down, row, row, row
row, row

RUM RUNNERS

Here is a taste of the great rum runners
Ships that sailed the velvet harbor
Crews that broke the jugs and poured
your blood like flowing rum upon the sand
sinking
    down, down, down
    upon the sand upon the sea
    upon the hills of liquid green
    they rise to fall
    they rise again
    Their dreams tattered sails
    in the wind

Here is the wail of a lone flute playin'
Those not hanged, by time were slain
Here is a cup of blood and tears
Here is the wall of a hundred years
going
    down, down, down
    upon the sand upon the sea
    upon the hills of liquid green
    they rise to fall
    they rise again
    Their dreams tattered sails
    in the wind

Overnight they turned to water
No blood ran when they went to slaughter
Tears were few, though sighs were heavy
Bones were stacked in the main library

Turning down, down, down
till their dreams are touching ground
Rising up like gentle rain
they turn to rise and fall again

Running round and changing faces
Marking time and keeping paces
Ducking down awhile to die
Their faces melt to barren sky

After all the trial and fury
They spared the judge and hanged the jury
No one asked the reason why
Sentence passed they turned to die

Turning down, down, down
till their dreams are touching ground
Rising up like gentle rain
they turn to rise and fall again

Here is fire and bloody slaughter
written on the leaves of water
Here is a ship with all hands singing
Here is a dock with dark men
swinging
    down, down, down
    upon the sand upon the sea
    upon the hills of liquid green
    they rise to fall, they rise again
    their dreams
    tattered sails
    in the wind

RUN FOR THE ROSES

Reach for the sun
Catch hold of the moon
They're both too heavy
but what can you do?
Reach for the stars
Smack into the sky
You don't want to live
but you're chicken to die
—chicken to die—

Run, run
Run for the roses
Sooner it opens
the quicker it closes
Man, oh, man
Oh friend of mine
All good things in all good time
All good things in all good time

Reach for the rose
Get caught on the briar
You're warming to love
Next thing there's a fire
The trouble with love
is its other face
You just want the cup
you don't want the race
No, you don't want the race . . .

Run, run
Run for the roses
Sooner it opens
the quicker it closes
Man, oh, man
Oh friend of mine

All good things in all good time
All good things in all good time

Run for the money
Caught short on the rent
Big ideas but
the money's all spent
If you got the do-re
I got the mi
And I got a notion
we're all at sea
Yeah, we're all at sea

Run, run
Run for the roses
Sooner it opens
the quicker it closes
Man, oh, man
Oh friend of mine
All good things in all good time
All good things in all good time

SAINT STEPHEN

Saint Stephen with a rose
In and out of the garden he goes
Country garland in the wind and the rain
Wherever he goes the people all complain

Stephen prosper in his time
Well he may and he may decline
Did it matter? Does it now?
Stephen would answer if he only knew how

Wishing well with a golden bell
Bucket hanging clear to Hell
Hell halfway 'twixt now and then
Stephen fill it up and lower down
and lower down again

Ladyfinger dipped in moonlight
Writing "What for?" across the morning sky
Sunlight splatters dawn with answers
Darkness shrugs and bids the day good-bye

Speeding arrow, sharp and narrow
What a lot of fleeting matters you have spurned
Several seasons with their treasons
Wrap the babe in scarlet covers, call it your own

Did he doubt or did he try?
Answers aplenty in the bye and bye
Talk about your plenty, talk about your ills
One man gathers what another man spills

Saint Stephen will remain
All he's lost he shall regain
Seashore washed in the suds and the foam
Been here so long he's got to calling it home

Fortune come acrawling, Calliope woman
Spinning that curious sense of your own
Can you answer? Yes, I can
But what would be the answer to the answer man?

High green chilly winds and windy vines in loops around the
twining shafts of lavender, they're crawling to the sun

Underfoot the ground is patched with climbing arms of ivy
wrapped around the manzanita, stark and shiny in the breeze

Wonder who will water all the children of the garden when they
sigh about the barren lack of rain and droop so hungry 'neath the
sky. . . .

William Tell has stretched his bow till it won't stretch no
furthermore and/or it may require a change that hasn't come
before

SCARLET BEGONIAS

As I was walking 'round Grosvenor Square
not a chill to the winter
but a nip to the air
from the other direction
she was calling my eye
Could be an illusion
but I might as well try
Might as well try

She had rings on her fingers and
bells on her shoes
I knew without asking she was
into the blues
Scarlet begonias
tucked into her curls
I knew right away
she was not like other girls—
other girls

In the thick of the evening
when the dealing got rough
she was too pat to open and
too cool to bluff
As I picked up my matches and
was closing the door
I had one of those flashes:
I'd been there before—
been there before

I ain't often right
but I've never been wrong
It seldom turns out the way
it does in the song
Once in a while
you get shown the light

in the strangest of places
if you look at it right

Well, there ain't nothing wrong
with the way she moves
Scarlet begonias or a
touch of the blues
And there's nothing wrong with
the love that's in her eye
I had to learn the hard way
to let her pass by—
let her pass by

The wind in the willows played tea for two
The sky was yellow and the sun was blue
Strangers stopped strangers
just to shake their hand
Everybody playing
in the Heart of Gold Band
Heart of Gold Band

SHAKEDOWN STREET

You tell me this town ain't got no heart
(Well, well, well—you can never tell)
The sunny side of the street is dark
(Well, well, well—You can never tell)
Maybe that's 'cause it's midnight
and the dark of the moon besides, or
maybe the dark is in your eyes
maybe the dark is in your eyes
maybe the dark is in your eyes
You know you got such dark eyes

Nothin' shakin' on Shakedown Street
used to be the heart of town
Don't tell me this town ain't got no heart
You just gotta poke around

You say you've seen this town clear through
(Well, well, well—you can never tell)
Nothin' here that would interest you
(Well, well, well—you can never tell)
It's not because you missed out
on the thing we had to start
Maybe you had too much too fast
Maybe you had too much too fast
Maybe you had too much too fast
and just overplayed your part

Nothin' shakin' on Shakedown Street
used to be the heart of town
Don't tell me this town ain't got no heart
You just gotta poke around

Since I'm passing your way today
(Well, well, well—You can never tell)
I just stopped in 'cause I want to say
(Well, well, well—You can never tell)
I recall your darkness
when it crackled like a thunder cloud

don't tell me this town ain't got no heart
don't tell me this town ain't got no heart
don't tell me this town ain't got no heart
when I can hear it *beat out loud*

Nothin' shakin' on Shakedown Street
used to be the heart of town
Don't tell me this town ain't got no heart
You just gotta poke around

SHE GIVES ME LOVE

I know she's not as pretty as you
Her hair's not wavy or her eyes so blue
but she gives me one thing
you don't never do
She gives me love
Ah, she gives me love

You know in a world like this
that's a pretty hard thing to do
I guess that's why I stay by her
though she may not be as fine as you
She gives me love
Ah, she gives me love

I know she can't compare with you
She don't even know me as well as you do
But she knows what I need
and she does come through
She gives me love
Ah, she gives me love

You know in a world like this
that's a pretty hard thing to find
So I guess I'm gonna stick by her
and leave the rest behind
She gives me love
Ah, she gives me love

I know she's not as pretty as you
Her hair's not golden and her eyes aren't blue
but she does one thing
you don't ever do
She gives me love
Ah, she gives me love

You know that the world outside
can be a pretty cold place to be
She knows how to keep it warm
and that means a lot to me
She gives me love
Ah, she gives me love
She gives me love

SHINING BLUE SEA

Green in the valley and margins between
Green along green along green
May I go faster? Yes you may go
To the edge of the shining blue sea

May I go slower? Yes you may go
But never more slowly than me
Stay by your shadow till daylight is done
By the edge of the shining blue sea

Jackie boy! Master?
How do you fare?
I fare pretty much as I please
Roll with the waves
and ebb with the tide
by the edge of the shining blue sea

Stand by the shadow you cannot outrun
Though your footsteps be ever so fleet
I will go with you wherever the sun
Reflects on the shining blue sea

May I go darkly in midnight, no moon
Nor hint of a light in the east?
I cannot stop you, go it alone
Even a shadow must sleep

Jackie boy! Master?
How do you fare?
I fare pretty much as I please
Roll with the waves
and ebb with the tide
by the edge of the shining blue sea

May I come back here? No you may not
Your days have delivered your deed
Go you alone and find you a home
In the deep of the shining blue sea

Green in the valley and margins between
Green along green along green
May I go faster? Yes you may go
To the edge of the shining blue sea

SHIP OF FOOLS

Went to see the captain
strangest I could find
Laid my proposition down
Laid it on the line;
I won't slave for beggar's pay
likewise gold and jewels
but I would slave to learn the way
to sink your ship of fools

Ship of fools
on a cruel sea
Ship of fools
sail away from me

It was later than I thought
when I first believed you
now I cannot share your laughter
Ship of Fools

Saw your first ship sink and drown
from rocking of the boat
and all that could not sink or swim
was just left there to float
I won't leave you drifting down
but—whoa!—it makes me wild
with thirty years upon my head
to have you call me child

Ship of fools
on a cruel sea
Ship of fools
sail away from me

It was later than I thought
when I first believed you
now I cannot share your laughter
Ship of Fools

The bottles stand as empty
as they were filled before
Time there was and plenty
but from that cup no more
Though I could not caution all
I yet may warn a few:
Don't lend your hand to raise no flag
atop no ship of fools

Ship of fools
on a cruel sea
Ship of fools
sail away from me

It was later than I thought
when I first believed you
now I cannot share your laughter
Ship of Fools
No I cannot share your laughter
Ship of Fools

SILVIO

Stake my future on a hell of a past
Looks like tomorrow is coming on fast
Ain't complaining 'bout what I got
Seen better times, but who has not?

Silvio, Silver and gold
Won't buy back the beat
of a heart grown cold
Silvio, I gotta go
Find out something
only dead men know

Honest as the next jade rolling that stone
When I come knocking don't throw me no bone
I'm an old boll weevil looking for a home
If you don't like it you can leave me alone

I can snap my fingers and require the rain
From a clear blue sky and turn it off again
I can stroke your body and relieve your pain
And charm the whistle off an evening train

Silvio, Silver and gold
Won't buy back the beat
of a heart grown cold
Silvio, I gotta go
Find out something
only dead men know

Give what I got until I got no more
I take what I get until I even the score
You know I love you and furthermore
When it's time to go you got an open door

I can tell you fancy, I can tell you plain
You give something up for everything you gain
Since every pleasure's got an edge of pain
Pay for your ticket and don't complain

Silvio, Silver and gold
Won't buy back the beat
of a heart grown cold
Silvio, I gotta go
Find out something
only dead men know

One of these days and it won't be long
Going down in the valley and sing my song
I will sing it loud, sing it strong
Let the echo decide if I was right or wrong

Silvio, Silver and gold
Won't buy back the beat
of a heart grown cold
Silvio, I gotta go
Find out something
only dead men know

(Bob Dylan released this as a single in 1988).

SLACK STRING QUARTET

Tune those strings down low as you can get
Add harp, bass, you got a slack string quartet
Barroom joy, relax and lose your face
It's such a dump, you can't trash the place

Slack String Quartet
What d'you think you get?
Sheer confusion!
Sheer confusion!

I had a cat I never could tame called
Collie in the Cauliflower Catalina Catalain
Roll Away the Butter Mama, Pepper on the Daisy Chain
Hairy Merry Salivary Singin' in the Rain—Wacko!

Slack String Quartet
What d'you think you get?
Sheer confusion!
Sheer confusion!

I reached in my pocket and shook hands with a thief
I said: Robbing me won't buy you much relief
Why don't you lend me twenty for a drink instead?
Set you down, let me tell you 'bout this life I led

You say your name is trouble, that's my name, too
I must be seeing double or I look like you
You say you're born to ramble, I was born to roam
An old boll weevil just seekin' his home-sweet-home

Slack String Quartet
What d'you think you get?
Sheer confusion!
Sheer confusion!

Hush, you screaming brat and I'll try to sing
Buy the Chase Manhattan for you and a bird with wings
If the bank goes broke, honey, and the bird gets smashed
Never mind, Daddy's still got him a backstage pass

For Slack String Quartet
What d'you think you get?
Sheer confusion!
Sheer confusion!

I had a dog I called for luck:
Isaiah Deuteronomy Ecclesiastes Habakkuk
Zephaniah Jeremiah Nehemiah Malachi
Samuel Zechariah Obadiah Do or Die

Slack String Quartet
What d'you think you get?
Sheer confusion, vain delusion
Cut and contusions—
Resolution, execution
Anything but some solution
Split it down the middle
Maybe even give a little
Collect, reject, suspect
Oh, Hell, what the heck
It it lands on its feet
without losing a beat
treat it to some respect:
Slack String Quartet!

THE SONG GOES ON

Hound and the kitty walked hand in hand
A full moon giddy and slick
Washed upon the Koconino sand
When out of the shadows there flew a brick
Kitty declared undying love
The mouse wound up in jail
Hound rolled in at ten to six
with lipstick on his tail

The song goes on—the song goes on
All night long the song goes on

Thigh bone said to shin bone
Meet me at the knees
We'll find someone to kick around
and something sweet to squeeze
Let's go down to lonesome town
and boogie till we die
Find someone to follow you down
Or find someone to try

The song goes on—the song goes on
All night long the song goes on

She cried: *Catch me if you can*
And ran ahead full speed
I was crushed in several pieces
In my heart if not in deed
I don't know where I got off
In attempting to get on
The Queen of Wild Horses
Who was pulling up the dawn

The song goes on—the song goes on
All night long the song goes on

Standing by the riverside
we shall not be moved
Until the situation is
very much improved
The song goes on and on and on
and on and on and on
From Gypsy campfire's midnight
Golden earrings into dawn

The song goes on—the song goes on
All night long the song goes on

Hearts are made for breaking
Tears made to be shed
Faith is made for shaking
Children to be fed
If there is no encore
Relax and let it be
The song goes on, that I know
The rest I must believe

The song goes on—the song goes on
All night long the song goes on
The song goes on—the song goes on
All night long the song goes on

STANDING AT YOUR DOOR

Here I'm standing at your door
like so many times before
since the time you let me in
I knew that I'd be here again

You know I know I've got no hope
Still I'm pulling at your rope
Once I thought I saw your face
peeking through your window lace

I know I know I saw your face
peeking through your window lace

Before I crawl back in the wall
Just what matters after all?
If the time and place are right
why not get it straight tonight?

When tomorrow comes around
there'll be time to melt it down
See what your tests of fire prove
Right now I can hardly move

Then you say that I tell lies
Won't believe a word I say

If you want to hear a song
I'll sing the only one I know
Steal a change and cop a rhyme
that I heard somewhere before

But please don't ask me to admit
what I been singing in the ditch
Where all these tunes that go around
have all been driven in the ground

Might as well be telling lies
You don't hear one word I say

Don't even know if it's a love song
Don't even know your left from wrong
Fact, the only thing you *do* know
is when it looks like time to go

So I'm standing at your door
Like so many times before
I know this time could be the last
if I don't get moving fast

I know I know I saw your face
peeking through your window lace
I heard you say the time will come
when there won't be
no place to run

And so I'm standing at your door
Like so many times before
Since the time you let me in
I knew that I'd be here again

I knew that I'd
be here
again

STANDING ON THE MOON

Standing on the moon
I got no cobweb on my shoe
Standing on the moon
I'm feeling so alone and blue
I see the Gulf of Mexico
As tiny as a tear
The coast of California
Must be somewhere over here
Over here

Standing on the moon
I see the battle rage below
Standing on the moon
I see the soldiers come and go
There's a metal flag beside me
Someone planted long ago
Old Glory standing stiffly
Crimson, white, and indigo
Indigo

I see all of Southeast Asia
I can see El Salvador
I hear the cries of children
And the other songs of war
It's like a mighty melody
That rings down from the sky
Standing here upon the moon
I watch it all roll by
All roll by

Standing on the moon
With nothing else to do
A lovely view of heaven
But I'd rather be with you

Standing on the moon
I see a shadow on the sun
Standing on the moon
The stars go fading one by one
I hear a cry of victory
And another of defeat
A scrap of age-old lullaby
Down some forgotten street

Standing on the moon
Where talk is cheap and vision true
Standing on the moon
But I would rather be with you
Somewhere in San Francisco
On a back porch in July
Just looking up to heaven
At this crescent in the sky

Standing on the moon
With nothing left to do
A lovely view of heaven
But I'd rather be with you
Be with you

STELLA BLUE

All the years combine
they melt into a dream
A broken angel sings
from a guitar
In the end there's just a song
comes crying like the wind
through all the broken dreams
and vanished years

Stella Blue

When all the cards are down
there's nothing left to see
There's just the pavement left
and broken dreams
In the end there's still that song
comes crying like the wind
down every lonely street
that's ever been

Stella Blue

I've stayed in every blue-light cheap hotel
Can't win for trying
Dust off those rusty strings just
one more time
Gonna make 'em shine

It all rolls into one
and nothing comes for free
There's nothing you can hold
for very long
And when you hear that song
come crying like the wind
it seems like all this life
was just a dream

Stella Blue

(Written at the Chelsea Hotel in 1970)

SUGAREE

When they come to take you down
When they bring that wagon round
When they come to call on you
and drag your poor body down

Just one thing I ask of you
Just one thing for me
Please forget you knew my name
My darling Sugaree

Shake it, shake it, Sugaree
Just don't tell them that you know me

You thought you was the cool fool
Never could do no wrong
Had everything sewed up tight
How come you lay awake all night long?

Just one thing I ask of you
Just one thing for me
Please forget you knew my name
My darling Sugaree

Shake it, shake it, Sugaree
Just don't tell them that you know me

You know in spite of all you gained
you still have to stand out in the
      pouring rain
One last voice is calling you
and I guess it's time you go

Just one thing I ask of you
Just one thing for me
Please forget you knew my name
My darling Sugaree

Shake it, shake it, Sugaree
Just don't tell them that you know me

Shake it up now, Sugaree
I'll meet you at the Jubilee
If that Jubilee don't come
Maybe I'll meet you on the run

One thing I ask of you
Just one thing for me
Please forget you knew my name
my darling Sugaree

Shake it, shake it, Sugaree
but don't tell them that you know me
Shake it, shake it, Sugaree
Just don't tell 'em that you know me

SUGAR MAGNOLIA/SUNSHINE DAYDREAM

Sugar Magnolia blossom's blooming
Head's all empty and I don't care
Saw my baby down by the river
Knew she'd have to come up soon for air

Sweet blossom come on under the willow★
We can have high times if you'll abide
We can discover the wonders of nature
Rolling in the rushes down by the riverside

She's got everything delightful
She's got everything I need
Takes the wheel when I'm seeing double
Pays my ticket when I speed

She come skimming through rays of violet
She can wade in a drop of dew
She don't come and I don't follow
Waits backstage while I sing to you

She can dance a Cajun rhythm
Jump like a Willys in four-wheel-drive
She's a summer love in the spring, fall, and winter
She can make happy any man alive

Sugar magnolia
Ringin' that blue bell
Caught up in sunlight
Come on out singing
I'll walk you in the sunshine
Come on, honey, come along with me

She's got everything delightful
She's got everything I need
A breeze in the pines in the summer night moonlight
Crazy in the sunlight, yes, indeed

Sometimes when the cuckoo's crying
When the moon is halfway down
Sometimes when the night is dying
I take me out and I wander round
I wander round

Sunshine daydream
Walk you the tall trees
Going where the wind goes
Blooming like a red rose
Breathing more freely
Light out singing
I'll walk you in the morning sunshine
Sunshine daydream
Walk you in the sunshine

★Lyrics in *italics* were written by Robert Weir.

211

SWEET LITTLE WHEELS

Sweet little wheels
ride so smooth you could say it had sex appeal
Patch of ice
glide right over it rides so smooth and nice
Hitch a ride?
Hop on in, it's got plenty of room inside
It's good on gas
What's more it's got plenty of power to pass

Sweet little wheels
Sweet-deet indeed
Sweet little wheels

What's your name?
What do you think of this light alloy frame?
What's your line?
Ain't built a car this solid since '49
Sakes alive
What other make and model would you
      want to drive?
Heighdy-hi
Don't forget to wave when you ride on by

Sweet little wheels
Sweet-deet indeed
Sweet little wheels

Forty/forty-five
fifty/fifty-five/sixty
Three-quarter throttle on a downhill curve
It'll go faster if you got the nerve
The rear holds in
even when you swerve

Sweet-deet indeed
Sweet little wheels

It's your lucky day
give you the keys, let you drive it away

One more thing
If you get work don't forget to write or ring
In the event
you get that car back here without a dent
we'll trade it in
on a big black shiny model with chrome and fins!

Sweet little wheels
Sweet-deet indeed
Sweet little wheels

TALKING MONEY TREE

Late last night layin' in bed
I found the answer to all my ills
A great big tree growing green and free
full of ten-thousand-dollar bills

Well, I went downtown to buy some wheels
Bought every car in town
Bought all the gas and all the oil
so we all could drive around

I bought the big department store
and everything inside
You could back up your truck and fill it up
The doors were open wide
      (It was company policy . . . we did it all the time)

I bought the park and I hired a band
to play every day for free
I bought the bars and the trolley cars
and the telephone company

You could call all day, say: *How's it goin?*
and never have to pay
Send telegrams to your wife and friends
saying: *You don't have to work today!*

But after a while I got so bored
I just gave the whole thing back
All I kept was a bar-and-grill
by the northbound railroad track

You can fall by here any time of night
or any time of day
The second cup of coffee's free
but the first one, you got to pay!

TELL ME IT WAS MAGIC

By a crocodile moon
In an alligator breeze
Blowing on a wishbone
Down upon your knees
Daylight over yonder
Fade the spell away
Tell me it was magic
That's all you have to say

Tell me it was magic
Not a feat of slight of hand
Tell me it was magic
I don't need to understand

Meet me in the middle
Rolling right along
Tell it like a riddle
Or sing it like a song
Seven cents a six pack
Best I could arrange
Take it for a nickel, babe
You can keep the change

Tell me it was magic
Not a feat of slight of hand
Tell me it was magic
I don't need to understand

When the pie was open
The birds began to shout
Mama sent a squad car
To find what it's about
Later in the courtroom
A ribbon in your hair
You told a tearful jury
That your baby wasn't there

Did you hide it up your sleeve
Or vanish it with mirrors?
I would just as soon believe
It's all that it appears
Tell them it was magic
Or they'll never understand
Tell them it was magic, babe
And play it to the stands

Tell me it was prophesied
And surely had to be
Don't tell how you manage it
It's no concern to me
Tell me it was magic
That's the only thing to do
Tell me it was magic
'Cause it might as well be true

TELL ME MAMA

Slip out of your shell, you said
Where else you got to go?
You been there and back again
What do you really know?

The saints each had his purpose
But you're not one of them
You are not the worst of fools
Nor yet the best of men

Oh—tell me Mama
Where did I go awry?
You know me best of anyone
You know how hard I try
You know how close I almost came
How far I fell away . . . but
I always kept you in my heart
Much more than I could say

Come and sit beside me
You can even tell me lies
It never was your honesty
It must have been your eyes

The way they looked inside me
Long ago and far away
While the snow was falling hard
From clouds of frozen gray

Oh—tell me Mama
Where did I go astray?
I tried as hard as anyone
To walk on feet of clay
You know the miles that lay between
The purpose and the deed . . . but
I always held you in my heart
Not just in time of need

Like some gypsy prophecy
The winds howl at my door
With fragments of my future
As I listen through the roar
Makes my blood run chilly
But enflames me to the core
If always means forever
I can take it one time more

All these broken promises
Assume some tight control . . . but
There never was no steering gear
And wheels just know to roll

Put the brake on gently
So the rubber will not burn
You been there and back again,
What did you really learn?

Oh—tell me Mama
Where did I go right?
To have you sit and talk to me
On this my needful night?
You know how much it means to me
I never could repay
I always kept you in my heart
Much more than I could say

TENNESSEE JED

Cold iron shackles and a ball and chain
Listen to the whistle of the evening train
You know you bound to wind up dead
if you don't head back to Tennessee, Jed

Rich man step on my poor head
When you get up you better butter my bread
Well, you know it's like I said
You better head back to Tennessee, Jed

Tennessee, Tennessee
There ain't no place I'd rather be
Baby, won't you carry me
Back to Tennessee

Drink all day and rock all night
Law come to get you if you don't walk right
Got a letter this morning and all it read:
You better head back to Tennessee, Jed

I dropped four flights and cracked my spine
Honey, come quick with the iodine
Catch a few winks down under the bed
Then head back to Tennessee, Jed

Tennessee, Tennessee
There ain't no place I'd rather be
Baby, won't you carry me
Back to Tennessee

I ran into Charley Phogg
He blacked my eye and he kicked my dog
My dog, he turned to me and he said:
Let's head back to Tennessee, Jed

I woke up a feeling mean
Went down to play the slot machine
The wheels turned round and
    the letters read:
Better head back to Tennessee, Jed

Tennessee, Tennessee
Ain't no place I'd rather be
Baby, won't you carry me
Back to Tennessee

("Tennessee Jed" originated in Barcelona, Spain. Topped up on *vino tinto*, I composed it aloud to the sound of a jaw harp twanged between echoing building faces by someone strolling half a block ahead of me in the late summer twilight.)

TESTIFY

Testify, testify,
I don't have to testify
I was not a witness to the crime, no
I was not a witness to the crime

You go ask some passerby
I don't have to testify
Yes, I heard the bullet fly
I saw no one fall and die

I was not a witness, no
I was not a witness, no
I was not a witness to the crime

Do you love me, do you not?
I just heard the pistol shot
Felt my blood run cold and hot
Spilling on the parking lot

What went down I really did not see
What went down I really did not see

Testify, testify,
I don't have to testify
I was not a witness to the crime
No, I was not a witness to the crime

Let me lie, let me lie
I don't need no alibi
The fault of this was none of mine
I was the victim of the crime

Testify, testify,
I don't have to testify
I was not a witness to the crime,
I was not a witness to the crime

THAT TRAIN

I see you standing at the station
with your undying hope in hand
You been standing there forever
Waiting for the midnight train to land
I sent a valentine to tell you
what you may have guessed before
But just in case you're still uncertain,
that train don't run here anymore

That train don't run here anymore
Not like it used to run before
When it brought Lady from the city
When it brought Stranger from the shore
Now it doesn't run here anymore
That train don't run here anymore

Polly, Polly, would you step
    inside the door?
Where you can't hear the howling
    of the train
If you don't look too hard at my decision
I'll never, never tease you again

You were confused by changing faces
Yeah, but when you learn the rules they
    change the game
You can catch the drift but not the drifter
He don't put his hand inside the flame
I see you hanging from a window
The very one you saw clear through before
You don't need no crystal ball to tell you
That train don't run here anymore

That train don't run here anymore
Not like it used to run before
When it brought gravy from the city
When it brought seashells from the shore
Now it doesn't run here anymore
That train don't run here anymore

Polly, Polly, would you step inside the
    door?
Where you can't hear the howling of the
    train
If you don't look too hard at my decision
I swear I'll never tease you again

You practiced hard at what you do
So when it came around it came to you
Anyone you want to take along
with half an ear could join in your song
But when that train gets busted open
to show an empty safe inside
you get slapped out of your slumber
to find that you don't have a face to hide

That train don't run here anymore
Not like it used to run before
Brought the big red apple to the city
and it even carted off the core
Now it doesn't run here anymore
That train don't run here anymore

THEY LOVE EACH OTHER

Merry run around
sailing up and down
just looking for a shove
in some direction—
got it from the top
it's nothing you can stop
Lord, you know they
made a fine connection
They love each other
Lord, you can see it's true

He could pass his time
'round some other line
but you know he
chose this place beside her
Don't get in the way
there's nothing you can say,
nothing that you need
to add or do
They love each other
Lord, you can see it's true

It's nothing they explain
It's like a diesel train—
you better not be there
when it rolls over
Though you make a noise
they just can't hear your voice,
they're on a dizzy ride
and you're cold sober
They love each other
Lord, you can see it's true

Heard your news report
Y'know you're falling short

Pretty soon won't trust you
for the weather
When their ship comes in
you won't know where it's been
Got to try to see
a little farther
They love each other
Lord, you can see that it's true

TIGER ROSE

Tiger Rose got new clothes,
the ladies love her so
They laugh at her connections
but they don't say no
Get down high, get down low
get your heels in tow
We don't care what
Mama don't allow here anymore

Tiger tea, tiger gee, you my Tiger Rose
Gently roll me, honey, while I sing your song
On the bank where the children play ring-a-levio
Come on and show me somethin' I don't know

Good day breaking, window shaking
at my cabin door
Love me like you did last night
just one time more
I know it don't make sense
but then it don't intend
If you keep coming by
we'll make it up again

Get up, Johnny, sing along,
get along now, get along
Could be right, I may be wrong,
pretty soon be long gone
Lay me down in worried sleep,
listen to the river weep
Thought I heard it sing a song
Delta Queen done come and gone

Tiger tea, tiger gee, you my Tiger Rose
Gently roll me, honey, while I sing your song
On the bank where the children play ring-a-levio
Come on and show me somethin' I don't know

Come on, big-eyed Handsome Moll
and be my party doll
We'll live in Jive-o county
'neath the waterfall
If people say: *What can you play?*
just tell 'em anything—
cut-glass spur or a silver chime,
can make 'em ring!

Tiger Rose, Heaven knows
I just love you so
Maybe that's the reason
that you don't say no
You get high, get down low
You my rodeo
We don't care what Mama don't allow here anymore

Tiger tea, tiger gee, you my Tiger Rose
Gently roll me, honey, while I sing your song
On the bank where the children play ring-a-levio
Come on and show me somethin' I don't know
Yeah, on the bank where the children play ring-a-levio
Come on and show me somethin'
Come on and show me somethin'
Come on and show me somethin' I don't know

TILL THE MORNING COMES

Till the morning comes
It'll do you fine
Till the morning comes
like a highway sign
Showing you the way
leaving no doubt
of the way on in
or the way back out

tell you what I'll do
I'll watch out for you
You're my woman now
Make yourself easy

Till we all fall down
It'll do you fine
Don't think about
what you left behind—
the way you came
or the way you go
Let your tracks be lost in the dark and snow

Tell you what I'll do
I'll watch out for you
You're my woman now
Make yourself easy

When the shadows grow
it'll do you fine
When the cold winds blow
it'll ease your mind
The shape it takes
could be yours to choose—
what you may win
what you may lose

Tell you what I'll do
I'll watch out for you
You're my woman now
Make yourself easy
Make yourself easy
Make yourself easy

You're my woman now, make
    yourself easy
You're my woman now, make
    yourself easy
You're my woman now, make
    yourself easy
You're my woman now, make
    yourself easy

TIN CROWN BLUE

Little glass of poison brew
killed my baby thru & thru,
that's why I'm blue
Wouldn't you be blue, too?

You say don't get discouraged
All it takes is time and courage
Lay long enough on the track
and the train will come

If I follow you all the way down
wearing the blues like an old tin crown
could you show me where to park?
Where to crash when it gets dark?

Sweet glory is the place that I come from
It's where I guess I'll go when I move on
Not asking for the seeds and core
but there's got to be some more
If you need someone to slam, I am your
        door

Shoot off the lock and tell you what I see
A stick, a string, and a leaf don't make a
        tree
    there's always one more rat to fleece,
    one more squeaky wheel to grease
    Good-bye, good luck, and please
    Sign this release

You say that's what friends are for
Might of been, it ain't no more
Take a lot of Auld Lang Syne
to square the score

Short of spitting in each other's eye
Let's just say that time does fly
Keep in touch and don't forget
to write me if you die

Sweet glory is the place that I come from
It's where I hope to go when I move on
Shift into overdrive, hit the brake
        when I arrive
Catch your death down here and think
        you're still alive

TIOGA PASS

Needle's on empty
and here I'm stuck
Four in the morning
and just my luck
Listen to the radio
waiting for the sun
Can't flag a ride
until daylight comes

Four in the morning
and out of gas
Mile and a half
from Tioga Pass

Tuned to a station
I've never heard
while moonlight glimmers
on Dead Man's Curve
Glory in the morning
and God bless you
for playing that song
when another would do

Four in the morning
and out of gas
Mile and a half
from Tioga Pass

Ain't quite rock
although it moves
It sure ain't country
and it's not the blues
They don't say nothing
when it gets to the end
Just keep playing it
over again

Four in the morning
and out of gas
Mile and a half
from Tioga Pass

It isn't pop
and it isn't soul
Nothing like fifties
rock and roll
It isn't folk
Not especially jazz
Got something special
nothing else has

Four in the morning
and out of gas
Mile and a half
from Tioga Pass

The sun comes up
about six o'clock
The station drifts
to some pre-fab rock
Although they played it
all night long
I never did learn
the name of that song

TO LAY ME DOWN

To lay me down
once more
To lay me down
with my head
in sparkling clover
Let the world go by
all lost in dreaming
To lay me down
one last time
To lay me down

To be with you
once more
To be with you
with our bodies
close together
Let the world go by
like clouds a-streaming
To lay me down
one last time
To lay me down

To lay me down
To lay me down
To lay me down
One last time
To lay me down

To lie with you
once more
to lie with you
with our dreams
entwined together
To lie beside you
my love still sleeping

to tell sweet lies
one last time
and say good-night

to lay me down,
to lay me down
to lay me down
one last time
to lay me down
to lay me down
one last time
to lay me down

TOUCH OF DARKNESS

Why does the rain fall
or the salt wind blow?
If you don't ask
you may never know

Ask no questions
you'll still hear lies
from the well intentioned
with stardust in their eyes

How good of you to love me
when my heart had been struck dumb
and the poisons of my anger
dripped staccato like a drum

How good of you to know me
when to touch me was to shame
yourself in front of everyone
In some obscure way to share my blame

Now, if I seem ungrateful
and my face a little hard
it's only that we both know
virtue was its own reward

In some cemetery midnight
underneath a wreath of rock
a living man awakens
and surveys his tomb in shock

How often do the dead wake
we thought were safely buried
With their secrets which would shake
the wind on which they're carried

With the shabby guilt and weakness
under which we all do live
that denounce you in the darkness
how dare you not forgive?

With each night so fully wretched
and its dawn so far from born
you slip so close to darkness
you could shake it by the horn

When morning does revive you
it revives a little less
of your hatred and your sorrow
your worst and of your best

Some may steal the prisons
that we leave because we go
If they fare ill or well there
it's not ours to care or know

Mmm . . . little touch of darkness
Dark and the deeper shades of gray
Mmm . . . momentary madness
This, too, will pass away

A TOUCH OF GREY

Must be getting early
Clocks are running late
Paint-by-number morning sky
Looks so phony

Dawn is breaking everywhere
Light a candle, curse the glare★
Draw the curtains
I don't care 'cause
It's all right

I will get by/I will get by
I will get by/I will survive

I see you've got your list out
Say your piece and get out
Yes, I get the gist of it
but it's all right

Sorry that you feel that way
The only thing there is to say
Every silver lining's got a
Touch of Grey

I will get by/I will get by
I will get by/I will survive

It's a lesson to me
The Ables and the Bakers and the Cs
The ABCs we all must face
And try to keep a little grace

It's a lesson to me
The deltas and the east and the freeze
The ABCs we all think of
Try to give a little love.

I know the rent is in arrears
The dog has not been fed in years
It's even worse than it appears
but it's all right.

Cows giving kerosene
Kid can't read at seventeen
The words he knows are all obscene
but it's all right

I will get by/I will get by
I will get by/I will survive

The shoe is on the hand it fits
There's really nothing much to it
Whistle through your teeth and spit
'cause it's all right.

Oh, well, a Touch of Grey
Kind of suits you anyway.
That was all I had to say
It's all right.

I will get by/I will get by
I will get by/I will survive
We will get by/We will get by
We will get by/We will survive

★(This line courtesy of Garcia.)

TOUGH CHANGES

Could be heaven hanging low
Now or never, who's to know?
Patience is a rich man's game
Backed up honking in your lane

Climb the ladder but like I said
Don't leave footprints on my head
Come down lightly when you tread
One man's gutter is another man's bed

Eeny-meeny-miney-mo
Could be the weather, I don't know
Tough changes and the winds do blow
Shit happens and away we go

All the textbook had to say
The rest of your life begins today
I don't care who gets the blame
Children are crying all the same

Tough changes in the parking lot
A broken bottle, a pistol shot
When the curtain falls this time
It falls on yours, it falls on mine

Shit happens, that's all we know
Shit happens and away we go
Tough changes—Wo-oah
You told me so I guess you know

Standing on the trapdoor spring
Hard to think about other things
Provocation from every side
Love, the law, and each other besides

Some of these days don't seem to end
Meet yourself coming 'round the bend
Shake your hand and slap your face
Keep your guard up just in case

Tough changes, look out below
Shit happens and away we go
Tough changes and the wind do blow
You told me so I guess you know

Keep it clean or keep it hid
Others fall for what you did
A hundred years on down the line
Will any part of our lovelight shine?

Tough changes, look out below
Shit happens and away we go
Tough changes and the wind do blow
Could be the weather, I don't know

TRUCKIN'

Truckin'—got my chips cashed in
Keep Truckin'—like the doodah man
Together—more or less in line
Just keep Truckin' on

Arrows of neon and flashing marquees out on Main Street
Chicago, New York, Detroit, it's all on the same street
Your typical city involved in a typical daydream
Hang it up and see what tomorrow brings

Dallas—got a soft machine
Houston—too close to New Orleans
New York—got the ways and means
but just won't let you be

Most of the cats you meet on the street speak of True Love
Most of the time they're sittin' and cryin' at home
One of these days they know they gotta get goin'
out of the door and down to the street all alone

Truckin'—like the doodah man
once told me you got to play your hand
sometime—the cards ain't worth a dime
if you don't lay 'em down

Sometimes the light's all shining on me
Other times I can barely see
Lately it occurs to me
What a long strange trip it's been

What in the world ever became of sweet Jane?
She lost her sparkle, you know she isn't the same
Living on reds, vitamin C, and cocaine
all a friend can say is "Ain't it a shame"

Truckin'—up to Buffalo
Been thinkin'—you got to mellow slow
Takes time—you pick a place to go
and just keep Truckin' on

Sitting and staring out of a hotel window
Got a tip they're gonna kick the door in again
I'd like to get some sleep before I travel
but if you got a warrant I guess you're gonna come in

Busted—down on Bourbon Street
Set up—like a bowling pin
Knocked down—it gets to wearing thin
They just won't let you be

You're sick of hanging around and you'd like to travel
Tired of travel, you want to settle down
I guess they can't revoke your soul for trying
Get out of the door—light out and look all around

Sometimes the light's all shining on me
Other times I can barely see
Lately it occurs to me
what a long strange trip it's been

Truckin'—I'm goin' home
Whoa-oh, baby, back where I belong
Back home—sit down and patch my bones
and get back Truckin' on

UGLIEST GIRL IN THE WORLD

The woman that I love, she got a hook in her nose
Her eyebrows meet, she wears secondhand clothes
She speaks with a stutter and she walks with a hop
I don't know why I love her but I just can't stop

You know I love her
Yeah, I love her
I'm in love with the Ugliest Girl in the World

If I ever lose her I will go insane
I go half crazy when she calls my name
When she says bababababy I l-l-love you
There ain't nothing in the world that I wouldn't do

You know I love her
Yeah, I love her
I'm in love with the Ugliest Girl in the World

The woman that I love, she got two flat feet
Her knees knock together walking down the street
She cracks her knuckles and she snores in bed
She ain't much to look at but like I said

You know I love her
Yeah, I love her
I'm in love with the Ugliest Girl in the World

I don't mean to say that she got nothing goin'
She got a weird sense of humor that's all her own
When I get low she sets me on my feet
Got a five-inch smile but her breath is sweet

You know I love her
Yeah, I love her
I'm in love with the Ugliest Girl in the World

UNCLE JOHN'S BAND

Well, the first days are the hardest days,
don't you worry anymore
When life looks like Easy Street
there is danger at your door
Think this through with me
Let me know your mind
Whoa-oh, what I want to know,
is are you kind?

It's a Buck Dancer's Choice, my friend,
better take my advice
You know all the rules by now
and the fire from the ice
Will you come with me?
Won't you come with me?
Whoa-oh, what I want to know,
will you come with me?

Goddamn, well, I declare
Have you seen the like?
Their walls are built of cannonballs,
their motto is *Don't Tread on Me*
Come hear Uncle John's Band
by the riverside
Got some things to talk about
here beside the rising tide

It's the same story the crow told me
It's the only one he know—
like the morning sun you come
and like the wind you go
Ain't no time to hate,
barely time to wait
Whoa-oh, what I want to know,
where does the time go?

I live in a silver mine
and I call it Beggar's Tomb
I got me a violin
and I beg you call the tune
Anybody's choice
I can hear your voice
Whoa-oh, what I want to know,
how does the song go?

Come hear Uncle John's Band
playing to the tide
Come with me or go alone
He's come to take his children home
Come hear Uncle John's Band
by the riverside
Come on along or go alone
he's come to take his children home

U.S. BLUES

Red and white/blue suede shoes
I'm Uncle Sam/how do you do?
Gimme five/I'm still alive
Ain't no luck/I learned to duck

Check my pulse/it don't change
Stay seventy-two/come shine or rain
Wave the flag/pop the bag
Rock the boat/skin the goat

Wave that flag
Wave it wide and high
Summertime
Done come and gone
My, oh, my

I'm Uncle Sam/that's who I am
Been hidin' out/in a rock-and-roll band
Shake the hand/that shook the hand
Of P. T. Barnum/and Charlie Chan

Shine your shoes/light your fuse
Can you use/them ol' U.S. Blues?
I'll drink your health/share your wealth
Run your life/steal your wife

Wave that flag
Wave it wide and high
Summertime done
Come and gone
My, oh, my

Back to back/children shack
Son of a gun/better change your act
We're all confused/what's to lose?
You can call this song/the United States Blues

Wave that flag
Wave it wide and high
Summertime done come and gone
My, oh, my
Summertime done come and gone
My, oh, my

VALERIE

Hey, Valerie, baby, what's the matter with you?
I did all of the things that you wanted me to
I went downtown with my pocketknife
Cut your other man but I spared his life
Valerie, won't you be good to me?

Valerie, baby, what's the matter with you?
Come on, come on, baby, and tell me true
Hey, now, baby, what did I do?
I shot my dog 'cause he growled at you
Valerie, won't you be good to me?

Valerie, what's the matter with me?
I never, never done you no wrong
I sing the blues nearly all night long
Valerie, what's the matter with me?
You know I'd do anything you say
I can't understand why you tell me
"Please go away"

I ain't afraid of the cold, cruel world outside
No Chicken Little running from a falling sky
The only thing troubles me is you
If you leave me, what can I do?
Valerie, won't you be true to me?

You got me down on the knees of my shakin' feet
Can't play the blues, 'cause of you I drop the beat
Valerie, what's your complaint?
I try to be everything I ain't
Valerie, won't you be good to me?
Valerie, won't you be good to me?

WALKER AFTER MIDNIGHT

A walker after midnight
On the road to "Auld Lang Syne"
I have walked a crooked mile
And I have walked the line
Walked on desert pathways
In the shadow of the flood
Slipped & fell from mountain tops
And swam in my own blood

A walker after midnight/More than this I cannot say
A walker after midnight/And I met you on my way

A walker after midnight
In another kind of light
I do not trust to reason
And I cannot trust to sight
I do not trust to messengers
With bright & shining eyes
I do not trust the foolish
And I dare not trust the wise

A walker after midnight/More than this I cannot say
A walker after midnight/And I met you on my way

A walker in the shadows
Between the walls of night
I used to thirst for glory
But I lost the appetite
Always one more trophy
I could never quite achieve
I'll settle for my sanity
And something to believe

Something to believe in
To the bottom of my soul
Something to hang on to
Something to console
Something to live up to
In spite of all disgrace
When all my other failings
Are paraded in my face

Maybe it's my destiny
To love what others hate
Maybe there is time to change
And maybe it's too late
At times I feel a light divine
And try to catch a spark
End up striking matches
Just to better see the dark

A walker after midnight/More than this I cannot say
A walker after midnight/And I met you on my way

A walker after midnight
And my destiny is grim
Staring at the starlight
till my eyes are growing dim
I still see well enough to know
The path I must pursue
If we meet again before the end
I'll share my fate with you

WEST L.A. FADEAWAY

Looking for a château
Twenty-one rooms but one will do
Looking for a château
Twenty-one rooms but one will do
I don't want to buy it
I just want to rent it for an hour or two

I met an old mistake
Walking down the street today
I met an old mistake
Walking down the street today
I didn't want to be mean about it
But I didn't have one good word to say

West L.A. Fadeaway
West L.A. Fadeaway
Little red light on the highway
Big green light on the speedway, hey, hey, hey

I had a steady job
Hauling items for the mob
I had a steady job
Hauling items for the mob
Y'know the pay was pathetic
It's a shame those boys couldn't be more copacetic

I meet a West L.A. girl
Already know what I need to know
I meet a West L.A. girl
I already know what I need to know
Name, address, and phone number
Lord, and just how far to go

West L.A. Fadeaway
West L.A. Fadeaway
Little red light on the highway
Big green light on the speedway, hey, hey, hey

Here's what Ginger says
She walks right, she ain't nobody's fool
Here's what Ginger says
She always tries to play by the golden rule
She says if you treat other people all right
Other folks probably treat you right, too

Looking for a château
Twenty-one rooms but one will do
Looking for a château
Twenty-one rooms but one will do
I don't want to rent it
I just want to use it for a minute or two

West L.A. Fadeaway
West L.A. Fadeaway
Little red light on the highway
Big green light on the speedway, hey, hey, hey

WHARF RAT

Wharf rat down
way down
down by the docks of the city,
Blind and dirty
asked me for a dime—
dime for a cup a coffee
I got no dime but
I got time to hear his story:

My name is August West
and I love my Pearly Baker best
more than my wine
   . . . more than My wine
more than my maker
though He's no friend of mine

Everyone said
I'd come to no good
I knew I would
Pearly believed *them*

Half of my life
I spent doing time for
some other fucker's crime
Other half found me stumbling around
drunk on burgundy wine

But I'll get back
on my feet someday
the good Lord willing
if He says I may
'cause I know the life I'm
living's no good
I'll get a new start
and live the life I should

I'll get up and fly away
  I'll get up and
fly away . . .
. . . fly away

Pearly's been true
true to me, true to my dying day
  he said
I said to him:
I'm sure she's been
I said to him:
I'm sure she's been true to you

I got up and wandered
Wandered downtown
nowhere to go
just to hang around
I got a girl
named Bonny Lee
I hope that girl's been true to me
I know she's been
I'm sure she's been
true to me

WHAT'LL YOU RAISE?

Met the lady face to face
who rules the joker and commands the ace
Just rolled in from the golden state
a dusty spoke on the wheel of fate

What'll you raise
What'll you raise
What will you raise
to stay in the game?

The only hand I hold is the hand I play
If I don't win it'll stay that way
Won't never know if I don't call
You could be bluffing, baby, after all

What'll you raise
What'll you raise
What will you raise
to stay in the game?

I follow the breeze
The quick autumn leaves
Who can deliver us all?
Is there a reaping
Or any safekeeping?
If not how far can we fall?
How far can we fall?

What'll you raise
What'll you raise
What will you raise
to stay in the game?

South of the moon, north of the sun
Cards on the table, it's one to one

Maybe our love was meant to be
Only way to find out is pay and see

What'll you raise
What'll you raise
What will you raise
to stay in the game?

Dive for diamonds or shoot for hearts
It's all uncertain but that's the art
I never bet on any sure thing
since your five deuces beat my four kings

What'll you raise
What'll you raise
What will you raise
to stay in the game?

What'll you pay
What'll you pay?
You'll have to pay
to stay in the game

What'll you raise
What'll you raise
What will you raise
to stay in the game?

WHAT'S BECOME OF THE BABY?

Waves of violet go crashing and laughing
Rainbow-winged singing birds fly 'round the sun
Sunbells rain down in a liquid profusion
Mermaids on porpoises draw up the dawn

What's become of the baby
This cold December morning?

Songbirds
frozen in their flight
drifting to the earth
remnants of forgotten dreaming
Calling . . .
answer comes there none
Go to sleep, you child
Dream of never-ending always

Panes of crystal
Eyes sparkle like waterfalls
lighting the polished ice caverns of Khan
But where in the looking-glass fields of illusion
wandered the child who was perfect as dawn?

What's become of the baby
this cold December morning?

Racing
rhythms of the sun
all the world revolves
captured in the eye of Odin
Allah
Pray, where are you now?
All Mohammed's men
blinded by the sparkling water

Scheherazade gathering stories to tell
from primal gold fantasy petals that fall
But where is the child
who played with the sun chimes
and chased the cloud sheep
to the regions of rhyme?

Stranded
cries the south wind
Lost in the regions of lead
Shackled by chains of illusion
Delusions of living and dead

THE WHEEL

The wheel is turning and you can't slow down
You can't let go and you can't hold on
You can't go back and you can't stand still
If the thunder don't get you, then the lightning will

Won't you try just a little bit harder?
Couldn't you try just a little bit more?
Won't you try just a little bit harder?
Couldn't you try just a little bit more?

Round, round robin, run around
Gotta get back where you belong
Little bit harder, just a little bit more
Little bit farther than you've gone before

Won't you try just a little bit harder?
Couldn't you try just a little bit more?
Won't you try just a little bit harder?
Couldn't you try just a little bit more?

Small wheel turn by the fire and rod
Big wheel turn by the grace of God
Every time that wheel turn 'round
bound to cover just a little more ground

Won't you try just a little bit harder?
Couldn't you try just a little bit more?
Won't you try just a little bit harder?
Couldn't you try just a little bit more?

The wheel is turning and you can't slow down
You can't let go and you can't hold on
You can't go back and you can't stand still
If the thunder don't get you, then the lightning will

Won't you try just a little bit harder?
Couldn't you try just a little bit more?
Won't you try just a little bit harder?
Couldn't you try just a little bit more?

WHEELS THAT SPIN

I got wheels that spin and wheels that walk
whispering grass and trees that talk
Chin down in my pocket
Little run-down at the heel
Ask how I'm doin', I say okay
but this is how I feel

When that train
goes rolling by
Sometimes when that train
goes rolling by
and it don't take me
it makes me want to cry

I feel better than I did the day before
Got the DT blues and I nearly bought the store
Saw a rainbow made of brick and steel
sharp as a butcher knife
I said: *Oh, no, can this be real?*
It said: *You bet your life*

When that train
goes rolling by
Sometimes when that train
goes rolling by
and it don't take me
it makes me want to cry

I got wheels that bark and wheels that bite
Things that crawl upon my skin all night
Got the gin down in my sockets
blowin' out my lights
Dark side of the moon shines
for me that's much too bright

When that train
goes rolling by

Sometimes when that train
goes rolling by
and it don't take me
it makes me want to cry

It's one-fifty-nine-fifty-nine, it's two o'clock
I got wheels that spin and wheels that walk
Baby, come and save me
Oh, don't be too long
I'll try to behave me
You know my love is strong

But sometimes when that train
goes rolling by
Sometimes when that train
goes rolling by
and it don't take me
it makes me cry
and it don't take me
it makes me
want to cry

WHEN A MAN LOVES A WOMAN

When you cross the sea of emotion
In a boat with no passenger side
Throwing all sense of precaution
To the waves to be lapped with the tide
With the west pouring sun in your eyes
Like the note of a bell from the blue
Granting keys to the moon and the sky
And it means less than nothing to you

When a man loves a woman
The way I love you
Nothing else matters
The way that you do

When you sweat from the face for a living
To retain some semblance of pride
And the work of your hands is a highway
Or a car in which you'll never ride
When the management threatens a layoff
And the union is striking for rights
And your benefit claim is rejected
Though the pain wakes you up in the nights

When a man loves a woman
The way I love you
Nothing else matters
The way that you do

When you fail to live up to your promise
And you falter so far from your dreams
And you have no distinction or honors
And your best coat is frayed at the seams
As long as your lovelight is burning
The house can collapse to the ground
As long as the world is turning
As long as she is still around

When a man loves a woman
The way I love you
Nothing else matters
The way that you do

When a man writes a love song
And I don't mean a construct of rhyme
But a couple of lines where his heart talks
Seeming perfectly clear at the time
Offers it up for your favor
Instead of a diamond bouquet
Don't ask what he means by forever
Accept that he mean it today

When a man loves a woman
The way I love you
Nothing else matters
The way that you do

(Unbelievable as it sounds, the existence of the classic 1966 Calvin Lewis–Andrew Wright song of the same title was unknown to me when I wrote this piece, although it has since become universally known through its use in several major ad campaigns.)

WHEN PUSH COMES TO SHOVE

Shaking in the forest, what have you to fear?
Here there may be tigers to punch you in the ear
Blades of stainless steel, bats carved out of brick,
Knock you down and beat you up and give your ass a kick
When Push Comes to Shove, you're afraid of love

Shaking in the desert, wherefore do you cry?
Here there may be rattlesnakes to punch you in the eye
Shotguns full of silver, bullets made of glass,
String barbed wire at your feet and do not let you pass
When Push Comes to Shove, you're afraid of love

When Push Comes to Shove
When Push Comes to Shove
You're afraid of love
When Push Comes to Shove

Shaking in the bedroom, covers on your head
Cringing like a baby at the hand beneath the bed
Phantom in the closet, scratching at the door
The latest mystery killer that you saw on Channel Four
When Push Comes to Shove, you're afraid of love

Shaking in the garden, the fear within you grows
Here there may be roses to punch you in the nose
Twist their arms around you, slap you till you cry,
Wrap you in their sweet perfume and love you till you die
When Push Comes to Shove, you're afraid of love

When Push Comes to Shove
When Push Comes to Shove
You're afraid of love
When Push Comes to Shove

WHEN THE LIGHTS WENT OUT

The party was over before I came in
Set up the tables and try it again
Call in the guests left hanging around
Give music to dance and a hammer to pound

By the side of the road on the highway to nowhere
We sit on a stone drinking wisdom and wine
Left here by somebody long lost before us
Few of us know or care what his name was

Over and over and over again
The same ages turning
The same pages burning

The sowers were sowing
The reapers were reaping
The singers were singing
Malingerers lingering

The shooters were shooting
Looters were looting
Believers believing
The doubters in doubt

But where, where, where in the world
Were you when the lights went out?

I opened my eyes and looked up from the ground
There was nobody near, there was no one around
Caught in the space between waking and dreaming
A heart full of fear and a head full of scheming

The party just started but I have to go
A knock at the door and wouldn't you know
If you detain me you'll only cause sorrow
I've nothing to lend you and nothing to borrow

Over and over and over again
The same wages earning
The same bridges burning

The children were crying
The liars were lying
The biters were biting
The bitten were writhing

The writers were writing
Confiders confiding
Believers believing
The doubters in doubt

But where, where, where in the world
Were you when the lights went out?
Where, where, where in the world
Were you when the lights went out?
Where in the world
Where in the world
Where in the world were you, my love,
Oh where in the world were you?
When the lights went out
When the lights went out
When the lights went out . . .

WHO, BABY, WHO?

Woke with the sun caught in my eye
under a pale and broken sky
The clouds painted ominous suggestions
while the wind asked one too many questions

Who, baby, who, baby, who?
You, maybe you, maybe you
Who, baby, who, baby, who?
You, maybe you, maybe you

Who was that lady on the train,
said: *So nice to see you again?*
Who was that rider in the rain
whose cool grey eyes were so full of pain?
Who was that writer in the night
trembling at the paper's virgin white?
Who was that child with a golden ball
playing catch with shadows in the hall?
Who was that lady on the train,
said: *So nice to see you again?*

Who, baby, who, baby, who?
You, maybe you, maybe you
Who, baby, who, baby, who?
You, maybe you, maybe you

Day is done and the clouds strike their sails
Shadows fall and the last rays of the sun fail
Stars appear with eyes of lucid fire
Shining with the sweet light of desire

Who was that man with the saxophone
playing like a band stood there all alone?
Who was that wrong number on the telephone
whose lovely laugh was severed by the dial tone?

Who was that stranger with a pocketknife
who carved his initials on the root of the tree of life?
Who left that silver silken veil
at the foot of the bed when morning dawned so pale?
Who was that lady on the train,
said: *So nice to see you again?*

Who, baby, who, baby, who?
You, maybe you, maybe you
Who, baby, who, baby, who?
You, maybe you, maybe you

Who was that girl in apartment B
who looked in the mirror, saw nothing but the sky and sea?
Who was that boy who believed in art
with the soul of a broken bottle and a broken heart?
Who was that face in knotty pine
on the wall of a cheap motel on Interstate 9?
Who was that rider in the driving rain
whose cool grey eyes were always so full of pain?
Who was that lady on the train,
said: *So nice to see you again?*

Who, baby, who, baby, who?
You, maybe you, maybe you
Who, baby, who, baby, who?
You, maybe you, maybe you

WILD BILL

In a torrid little cabin
'neath Aurora Boreeay
Wild Bill waxed his whiskers
dabbed perfume behind each ear
from a flask of Spanish lotion
that he'd had for many years
Kept it for occasions
when he went to see his dear
When he went down to see that little girl

Slipped off a ring of silver
Slipped on a ring of gold
with a twenty-carat diamond
that was carved into a rose
An ivory-stemmed revolver
was reflected in his boots
that glittered like the cuff studs
setting off his lovin' suit
when he went down to see that little girl

Threw a handful of ash on the fire
Made his way out through the snow
to the finest cuisine south of Canada
The finest north of Mexico
The lady who was his intention
with the look fit to fetch or to kill
had tattooed 'neath the lace on her bosom
"Wild Bill Loves Diamond Lil"

She was not just the girl of his dreams
He was not only fond of her charms
She could knock down a man at ninety paces
while he rolled her around in his arms
Shot a hole through the hand of Michael Miller
as he crept up behind Wild Bill

Said: *Now share a little of the life I saved you*
where you know you can relax and not get killed

Jacob nailed the ladder to the floor
Now we can't move the ladder 'round no more
Sunday is the day we go church and pray the Lord
will take us when we die to golden shores
Monday is the day we go to work and pay our bills
Saturday we go and spend what's left at Diamond Lil's
Yeah, that's the day we go to Diamond Lil's

In a torrid little cabin
'neath Aurora Boreeay
Wild Bill waxed his whiskers
dabbed perfume behind each ear
from a flask of Spanish lotion
that he'd had for many years
Kept it for occasions
when he went to see his dear
When he went down to see Diamond Lil

WILLY MORRIS

I'm a vagabond evangelist
with a mighty healing touch
I'm one-half fighting Irish
and one-half double Dutch
My name is Willy Morris
I preach the revelation
I'm a rough-and-ready rider
in the service of the Kingdom

When I call the power down
short men stand up taller,
the lame and halt kick up their heels,
the dumb begin to holler
Upon the stage I strut my stuff
with sanctifying grace
Righteousness within my soul
and rapture on my face

Don't turn away
Step up and see
what I can do
when you believe

I was born a Jersey boy
My folks had wealth and pull
One thing about good people
they do get dreadful dull
When I took up testifying
they said: *Don't bring us shame*
If you work this county, son,
be sure and change your name

The Lord wants you to dress in style
and drive the very best
Long as you take care of me,

I'll take care of the rest
One thing about the Kingdom,
since it's always Kingdom Come
I get by on *glory be*
plus tambourine and drum

Don't turn away
Step up and see
what I can do
when you believe

I'm honest as the people
who admit to being saved
yet grow as mean as any weed
on any beggar's grave
Squirm, you sinners, howl and moan
The Devil is your due
But if you will take care of me
I will take care of you

I'm a vagabond evangelist
with a mighty healing touch
I'm one-half fighting Irish
and one-half double Dutch
My name is Willy Morris
I preach the revelation
I'm a rough-and-ready rider
in the service of the Kingdom

Don't turn away
Step up and see
what I can do
when you believe
when you believe
when you believe

WILLY POOR BOY

The kind of face just a mother could love
The kind of a place where they give you a shove
and you wake in the morning in traction or worse,
one of those situations you can never rehearse
The kind of a bastard that Hell would reject
punched out your teeth and put a crease in your neck

Whoa, Willy poor boy
Out of luck today
Whoa, bad-luck Willy
What you got to say?

I'll give your regards to the beautiful girls
while you're getting patched up and back in the world
I'll see that your wife gets plenty of love
and any other thing that I can think of
'Cause I am your friend and I'm glad to oblige
I checked out your threads and they're about my size

Whoa, Willy poor boy
Out of luck today
Whoa, bad-luck Willy
What you got to say?

When you are all mended and back home again
I know you'll always remember your friend
Although you can't talk, only gurgle and wink
hey, Willy poor boy, I know what you think:
A friend in trouble is a friend indeed
and what you got here is a friend in need

Whoa, Willy poor boy
Out of luck today
Whoa, bad-luck Willy
What you got to say?

WOMAN IN WHITE

Across the hills by lamplight
Far away not long ago
Swearing softly to myself
Way down in Jericho
Making fifteen dollar bills
With you upon the face
I hope it was a dream but
I keep printing just in case

You told me to step inside
"Inside of what?" said I
"Here inside this dream of mine"
I said "you know I try"
Once inside you said "see this—
What does it mean to you?"
Parts were from a dream of mine
But most of it was new

A saintly woman all in white
Like vapor on the stair
Burst into a melody
That floated from her hair
I recall a snatch or two
It sounded like Saint Saëns
Played backwards on a mandolin
The strangest little song

The music was the least of it
It's what she sang about
Almost on the tongue tip but
Somehow it won't come out
The logic was persuasive
Like it always is in dream
Where everything is anything
Except what it may seem

I said "I had a dream like this
Myself some time ago
It seemed to be important but
With dreams you never know
Awoke and tried to write it down—
The entrance and the out
But all I wrote was nonsense
I can't tell what it's about

"I wonder if the things of life
Seem just as strange to dream
Where what you cannot face awake
Seems such a natural thing"
You poured a cup of moonbeam
And assumed a thoughtful face
Just such a look as angels have
Before they fall from grace

WOODSHED TIME

Down in the woodpile
fox meet a groundhog
Bid him fare-thee-well
It's a good morning
Old times here are
not forgot
We just lay around
and watch 'em rot

Take it to the woodshed
Woodshed time
Take it to the woodshed
Right now!

Tell me what you do
don't tell me what you don't know
Come around later
with *I told you so*
Mercy to the child
out in the cold
Engine cranks over
but the wheels won't roll

Take it to the woodshed
Woodshed time
Take it to the woodshed
Right now!

Tie it to a postcard
Freight it on a boxcar
Little Joe from Detroit
there you are
Betting on snake eyes
Twenty as the crow flies
Out in the woodshed
shooting high dice

Take it to the woodshed
Woodshed time
Take it to the woodshed
Right now!

Take it to the woodshed
Strip it down to pieces
Little touch of grease
Not too much, please
When I'm down to
my last fifty cents
I do love the lady
who pays the rent

Take it to the woodshed
Woodshed time
Take it to the woodshed
Right now!

Cross an alligator
with a sheep and a hound-dog
pick of the litter
won't amount to shit
Don't you worry 'bout
the little red rooster
He just laid an egg
and that's the end of it

WORRIED SONG

It takes a worried man
Four in the morning with a road map in his hand
It takes a worried man/
To summon the demon of love from a bottle
and I know you understand
It takes a worried man
To love someone who just don't give a damn
Worried man
To walk in on the woman he loves in the arms of another man
It takes a worried man—to sing a worried song

If I thought we had a chance
I'd stick around and sweat
Try to work the small stuff out
The other—just forget
I can't stand a long good-bye
So I'll just say: So long!
You know it takes a worried man
to sing a worried song

It takes a worried man
Nothing less to sing a worried song
It takes a worried man
To come to terms with the facts of life in the light of a cold grey dawn
Takes a worried man
Worried now but I won't be worried long
Worried man
I'd like to think
I got an open mind but you know I ain't that strong
Takes a worried man—to sing a worried song

Don't ask me to compromise,
Accept and learn to trust
You're only wasting words on me
I'm doing what I must
I can't do no other way
I been this way too long
You know it takes a worried man
to sing a worried song

It takes a worried man
Bed you made ain't wide enough for three
It takes a worried man
Oh, babe, I'm just gonna cut you free
Worried man
Worried now but I won't be worried soon
It takes a worried man
Devil rode out in the saddle of a full black moon
Takes a worried man . . . to sing a worried tune

YELLOW MOON

Anxious hope and thoughts of love
will never let me down or let me go
Inside my heart's a cage of ice
where love and loss still toss the lonely dice
I burned the whole night long
my thoughts were never far from you
Love that locks and binds must die
but when it does a bit of you goes, too

Born, born, born upon the world
the restless heart keeps flying
trying to become the heart of home
Love, love, love, it picks you up
and spins you round
sets you right back down where you belong

My head don't fit my hat sometimes
it gets so full of clouds
Every time I pass your door
I hear you cry out loud
Sometimes I look the same to you
as you have looked to me
My eyes get filled so full of stars
I don't know when to leave

Born, born, born upon the world
the restless heart keeps flying
trying to become the heart of home
Love, love, love, it picks you up
and spins you round
sets you right back down where you belong

Love is like the April rain
that makes the harvest grow
and when it grows it's
like the summer gold
Love is like the colored leaves
that drift down from the trees
one by one till every tale is told

If I go a-dancing out across the yellow moon
I'll be home by morning if it doesn't come too soon
If you seek protection go and find a safety man
If he can't give you what you need
then come on by again

Priestess of the sun and moon
and goddess of the wind
you know too much to ever lose
and not enough to win
Though you built your house upon the rock
and not upon the sand,
you still looking out your window
for another traveling man

Born, born, born upon the world
the restless heart keeps flying
trying to become the heart of home
and it's love, love, love picks you up
and spins you round,
sets you right back down where you belong
Yeah, it's love, love, love that picks you up
and spins you round
sets you right back down where you belong

SUITES

Alligator Moon

MESA LINDA

(The *Alligator Moon* suite was recorded but never released by the band Comfort in 1976. A ballet was choreographed for it and we performed the whole show three times, most notably at the Hooker's Ball—the last occasion of that peculiarly San Francisco annual celebration.)

Under cloak of midnight 'neath an alligator moon
all the way from Corpus Christi in a '50 Coupe de Ville . . .
Domino at the wheel, spelled by Cigarette,
me and Melina Marie low in the backseat
Do you know Domino? Have you met Cigarette?
Or Melina—especially Melina—she's kind of a dreamer

from Mesa Linda—lovely mountain
where she counts the falling stars outside her window

Alligator moon ascending in three-quarters round
shine down on Melina as she drives from town to town
Domino and Cigarette, Oh, grant them both an ivory throne
for never thinking twice about leaving well enough alone

leaving well enough alone
leaving well enough alone
leaving well enough alone
leaving well enough alone
leaving well enough alone
on the Mesa Linda

Alligator moon on the horizon
the sun is even having trouble rising
at last it finally gives a bloody glow
'round the time we pull into Arroyo Hondo

Melina breaks into a sigh
"This is where we say good-bye
Our paths may cross *via con Dios*—
It's been a long winter's night
but spring is well in sight
When it comes we'll have a party
in Arroyo Hondo"

Domino got handy
Tore up the place with a song
Cigarette, dark as night,
before the morning dawned
Melina lets it happen
You know she must've wrote the play
Had better luck in the roundabout
than in the right of way
but, Oh! Melina
I guess things happen that way

Oh! Leave well enough alone
Oh! Leave well enough alone
On Mesa Linda—lovely mountain
Where the moon and stars hang right down to your window
Mesa Linda—about an hour
as the crow flies south from Arroyo Hondo
Mesa Linda—such a lovely mountain
Why, you can count the falling stars outside your window
Mesa Linda—my wheels howl by
If I leave well enough alone
I'll live there someday!

Oh—leave well enough alone
Oh—leave well enough alone
Oh—leave well enough alone
Oh—leave well enough alone on the Mesa Linda

DOMINO, CIGARETTE, AND MELINA

Domino, Cigarette, and Melina
took off in a dusty cloud
When I saw Melina waving bye-bye
You know I nearly cried out loud:

"Hey, Melina, Melina—
Hold on and wait for me!"
But I just stood by the side of the road
thinking what fools these mortals be

That's the story of my life
It might be the story of your life, too
That's the story of Domino, in small part,
Cigarette, and most surely Melina

High-roll shakin' and loving
Octane cola with a shot of rum
Sometimes I remember you, Melina
in the flash of a cymbal or the kick of a drum

Hey, Melina, Melina
Hold on and wait for me!
I'm still here by the side of the road
thinking what fools these mortals be

what fools
bye-bye
what fools
Melina, Melina . . .

DOMINO

As the crow flies south from Arroyo Hondo
As the crow flies south from Arroyo Hondo
Oh . . . Domino . . . Oh . . . Domino . . . Oh . . . Domino . . . Oh . . .

Domino was daughter to a fan-tan dancer
and an Albuquerque rancher
Melina and Johnny Low

There was green fire—static lightning
clinging to your cradle
the night you were born

If this was an omen
no one could say—but you
grew into a mighty lovely woman

On Mesa Linda
Lovely mountain
Well, I sure love your daughter Domino

Oh . . . Alouette . . . Oh . . . Cigarette . . . Oh . . . Alouette . . . Oh . . .

Domino met Cigarette
whose real name was Alouette
Cherry St. Hélène, a girl of French descent

who left St. Lou and met Melina 'cross the borderline
If beauty's in the beholder's eye
it must have been in mine

'cause when I saw Melina with you on either hand,
something in my heart stood
and played *strike up the band!*

Melina . . . Oh, Melina . . . Melina . . . Oh . . .

This was not the time or place to fall into romance
but I fell into three that night
and not one stood a chance

Cigarette, dark as night, 'neath an alligator moon
Domino, white as milk,
sang in perfect tune

Melina like a sunbeam in an ivory frame
Hey—Melina
I remember your name

Melina
from Mesa Linda
'bout an hour and a half from Arroyo Hondo

Oh . . . Domino . . . Oh . . . Domino . . . Oh . . . Domino . . . Oh . . .

There was green fire—static lightning
clinging to your cradle
the night you were born

When I first saw Domino with Cigarette 'longside
why, something in my heart stood
and said: *I'll take that ride*

Then I saw Melina
like a sunbeam in a frame
Hey, Melina . . . I remember your name

Melina
from Mesa Linda
about an hour and a half from Arroyo Hondo
Melina, ah, Melina
well, I sure love your daughter Domino

Domino, Domino
if not for Melina
I'd of stayed with you in Mesa Linda

Mesa Linda
Lovely mountain
about an hour and a half from Arroyo Hondo

As the crow flies south from Arroyo Hondo
As the crow flies south from Arroyo Hondo

BLUE NOTE

Ah, meet me, Mama, down at the *Blue Note*
Alligator moonlight, east of St. Lou
Ringing the old out to welcome the new
Sound and solid and possibly true

Born in an alley of Jazz America
Learned my blues from a crow on my cradle
Could be true—it might be a fable
Gonna believe it long as I'm able

Something for nothing
You can't never get   *(Answer-Back Dialogue)*
You gotta give sometime
But maybe not yet
Ain't in the mood for no serenata
Just a hard-rockin' vision of Jazz Am-er-aka
Blue-blue-blue note
Blow me away
No bright lights
Just a touch of shade
Climb to the stars on a hook and ladder
Who is it for? What does it matter!

Ah, meet me, Mama, down at the *Blue Note*
In alligator moonlight—it's all she wrote
I've honky-tonked 'round in my time
But East St. Lou is the end of the line

You say you got trouble
No complaint
You score like a sinner
Sleep like a saint
Dancing so sassy till quarter to three
To the scent of jasmine on the balcony
Playin' the blue-blue
Struttin' the strings
Does it matter?
Does anything?

Go for the feeling, that's all she wrote
Cut cross America down to the *Blue Note*

Whole new vision born every night
Smokey Joe's Café just off to the right
Eat when you're hungry—sleep when you're tight
Down here they only come out at midnight

Stash your coin purse before you go down
It ain't exactly a rich part of town
But they never swing right down on easy street
There's no substitute for a strong back beat

Meet me, Mama, down at the *Blue Note*
Alligator midnight, east of St. Lou
They're playin' so hot on the Blue Note Stage
Gotta keep the drummer locked in a cage

Rock-and-roll vision born every night
Incredibly sweet and just so right
Born in the alleys of Jazz America—singing
Down in East St. Lou
Born in the alleys of Jazz America—singing

NEW EAST ST. LOUIS BLUE

Cigarette—come tell me truly
Are you thinking of leaving St. Louis?
Down to the last inch of spike-heeled shoes
Singing the New East St. Louis Blue
It's all right—it don't matter
It's all right—it don't matter!

St. Louis Dispatch underneath your bed
A picture of your man and a headline which read:
Swing Low Johnny gets five to life
For carving his rival with a switchblade knife

What can you say?
Don't say nothing
He never treated you right anyway

It's all right—just the New East St. Louis Blue
Farewell—East St. Louis
All right—just the New East St. Louis Blue

Put on your red dress
Last good party gown
Put a ribbon in your hair
We'll go strolling downtown
Maybe there's someplace where
the music is loud and clear

Maybe the Blue Note down by the river
Maybe the Blue Note down by the river
Singing the New East St. Louis Blue
Farewell—East St. Lou
Singing the New East St. Louis Blue

You could cut out on a high wail
Ride the midnight blue—sail
South—south—down the Mississippi
A blue farewell to East St. Louis
Blue, blue, sail the blue
Claim it—frame it—make it come true

You know, Alouette, way down in your heart
If you don't go now, girl, you never will start
Cloak of rhythm rich as sable
Break on out, girl, you know you're able
Rock in the alley
Blue in the street
St. Louis girl sail away on the beat

All right—just the New East St. Louis Blue
All right—just the New East St. Louis Blue
All right, Alouette—all right, Cigarette
All right—just the New East St. Louis Blue
All right . . . Okay
All right—just the New East St. Louis Blue
It's all right—all right—Okay
Just the New East St. Louis Blue

A m a g a m a l i n   S t r e e t

INTRODUCTION

The idea for *Amagamalin Street* occurred to me while leaning against a building on Fifth Avenue. I was in one of those ego-flattened mindframes that visit my West Coast psyche when confronted by Manhattan.

I began thinking about the values people must assign to themselves, and believe in despite all evidence, in order to cope with the giganticism of Metropolis. I saw a drunk on the other side of the street making a show of himself—and I began inventing his story. I had a pencil but no paper—not a problem in New York; I picked up a handbill in the gutter for a show at the Apollo, and began to write on the back of it.

SYNOPSIS BY SONG:

ROSEANNE:

Chet, a smooth-talking, hard-drinking womanizer, awakens with a bad hangover to discover that Roseanne, his latest meal ticket, whom he has been living with for a few weeks in a cheap hotel, has walked out, leaving only a good-bye note. He figures she'll be heading home—somewhere down South—and hurries to the bus station to intercept her. It seems he'd smacked her around in his drunkenness of the night before, so he has a lot of fast talking to do. He pleads that he has seen the light, that they need each other, and, most important, that he has a good deal of money hung up in probate court, courtesy of an uncle who has just died. She agrees to run with him on the condition that he never again raise his hand against her.

It so happens that Roseanne has turned in the key to the hotel room and they spend the night riding the subway back and forth to Far Rockaway. They decide to spend what little Roseanne has left—the price of the bus ticket—on drugs, which Chet cuts twice and deals for ready cash to get to San Francisco in order to hang out until the will passes probate.

Once on the coast, in dire need of money, Chet convinces Roseanne that she has the gift of second sight (after all, he argues, "You see through me") and sets her up as a fortune-teller, relying on his glibness to bring in customers. Over a period of time, Roseanne becomes increasingly demoralized and drinks heavily as Chet gains more and more control of her, eventually pressuring her into prostitution.

One day, he disappears. He eventually calls her from New York to say that the will is finally being settled and that he will call again, which he does not do until a year later, after splitting up with his new girl, Maggie (this story is related in the next song: "Amagamalin Street"). In a characteristic fit of sentimentality, he tries to re-establish contact with Roseanne but cannot do so. He comforts himself with the thought that at least she can support herself with the profession to which he has introduced her.

277

AMAGAMALIN STREET:

After leaving Roseanne and returning to New York, two new characters enter Chet's life: Maggie, an ingenue from upstate who has succumbed to Chet's charms but retains enough free spirit to cause him uncomfortable jealousy; and his friend Murphy, a decent man who is relegated to the trash-heap of Amagamalin Street due to mental scars from his Vietnam tour, which have left him unable to cope with normal life.

Maggie, abused by Chet, finds a sympathetic friend in Murphy, who cannot help but fall for her. Chet sizes up the situation and, mistakenly believing that Maggie reciprocates Murphy's passion, relinquishes her, believing Murphy's friendship to be of more value—besides, he has no need for a woman to "live off," having finally received his uncle's inheritance.

This song anticipates some of the events that will be revealed later when Murphy tells his side of the story in Part Two, which begins with the song *Ithaca*.

GYPSY PARLOR LIGHT:

Deep in the throes of his alcoholic degeneration, Chet has a disturbing encounter with a beautiful young Gypsy fortune-teller who tells him that he has no future beyond his nightly partying. He tells Murphy, who, having grown up in that part of town, swears that there is no such Gypsy parlor as the one Chet describes. Chet takes him to the location but they discover only a vacant lot.

Returning to his room after a night of carousing, Chet takes a left where he "shoulda took a right" and discovers the Gypsy parlor again, closed. Demanding admittance, he finds the Gypsy mysteriously aged. He pays her the last hundred dollars left of his uncle's money in exchange for a frightening prophecy, then passes out. Next morning, he awakens shivering in a vacant lot.

Deranged by the experience, he tries desperately to convince others that it really happened, obsessively showing a piece of old wallpaper from the Gypsy parlor—discovered in his wallet in place of the hundred-dollar bill he paid the Gypsy—as proof.

RAMBLING GHOST:

Facing his own utter degeneration, yet still asserting his pride, Chet casts a sentimental eye back on his life and times, including the affair with Roseanne, and excuses himself from any blame for the bleak outcome of his existence.

ITHACA:

This begins Part Two, which is Murphy's narration. He speaks of Maggie and of the circumstances that, despite his friendship for Chet, caused him to try to win her away. This song begins a series of flashbacks that continues until the last song.

DON'T BE DECEIVED:

Finding Maggie badly beaten by Chet, Murphy attempts to wise her up to his friend's destructive nature: "I know him as a son of a gun but he's a son of a bitch with a woman."

TAKING MAGGIE HOME:

Murphy finally faces Chet down, in Maggie's presence, and vows that he will not let Chet destroy her. Maggie agrees to come with him.

OUT OF THE CITY:

Murphy tries to persuade Maggie that their only chance for a decent life is to get the hell out of the city.

BETTER BAD LUCK:

They make their break for a better life, but Murphy's '49 Ford gets them only as far as the Catskills before breaking down. He resigns himself, philosophically, by saying that their luck is not as bad as it could be: "[We] coulda broke down in the Lincoln Tunnel halfway to Jersey."

STREETWISE:

Back on Amagamalin Street, their escape attempt proving a washout, Murphy finds Maggie growing more and more distant. She has lost the innocence that first attracted him to her and appears to be fast becoming another streetwise casualty of skid row.

FACE ME:

Alerted by her bruises, Murphy realizes that Maggie has been secretly seeing Chet again. He angrily demands that she face him with the truth—and that she look at the truth herself. He admits that she could do better than a war casualty like himself—that his only concern at this point is that she not allow herself to be dragged to destruction by her morbid fascination for Chet.

WHERE DID YOU GO?

Maggie leaves Murphy. In this soliloquy, he speaks of the emptiness of his existence without her.

13 ROSES:

Several years after the disappearance of Maggie and the death of Chet, Murphy meets Roseanne. He tells her of Chet's passing but doesn't give her the details—saying only that Chet spoke highly of her at the end. A spark is kindled between the two as the present bids to replace the ghosts of the past.

ROSEANNE

Woke out of a dream
gold hearts with bat wings
pouring out of my throat
Now, what's this note?
Oh, no! Roseanne
She's walked out on me
Ain't that sweet?
. . . walked out on me

What's wrong with that girl?
Head in another world
Here I sit in Rat City
Hotel and no pity
Roseanne—Look how you treat your man
Roseanne—You don't understand

Bet she's packing her stuff
Planning to catch a bus
I think she's Southern, I didn't ask
I'll check the station

I'll hit the deck and wail
use the method that don't fail
Say it so she's gotta believe
Fall on my hands and knees and cry:
Please
Roseanne
Roseanne
Don't fall out on me

Get out of my life
Get out for good, Chet
Get off of your knees
I'll call the police
Roseanne, this can't be true
Think of what we been through
I know I've thrown a curve or two
but I deserve

better from you
You know I do
Roseanne
I want to be your man

I'm sick, my head hurts
Watcha got in your purse?
Empty wallet and gum
Pint of Cuban rum
High heel offa my shoe
Map of Atlanta, what's it to you?
What's the name of the book?
Take it and have a look

"Our Hearts Had Wings"
hmm
hahaha

Romance from the market rack
Roseanne, what trash
Back off, I read what I like
Come on, now, get out of my life
. . . out of my life

Guess I got no basis to doubt
I'll read it myself and find out
Forget it, I found it in the street
A cold wind rippled its leaves
. . . rippled its leaves

You complain if I think or
step out to have a drink
You finally took a swing at me
and man, that's over the line
Don't waste my time
I was raised in that scene
It won't happen to me

Roseanne, remember the day
We swore our love would never decay?

Down on the avenue under the el
It rained hearts and flowers fell
Didn't they fall?
Hearts, flowers, and all
Didn't they fall . . .

C'mon, Roseanne, let's try it again
UNH-UH—you don't understand
This is my moment of truth
If I come back I'll never pull loose
Don't you see?
I'll never pull free
. . . never pull free

Roseanne, I'm on my knees
Please
don't
fall out on me
I want to be your man
Roseanne
I know I can

You need me to stand behind
Babe, you're not the tough kind
Me, I hustle, I ain't shy
We go together, you and me
It's chemistry
Roseanne
You belong to me!

Remember my uncle who went bail
when I was busted for blackmail?
Well, he's gone to his reward
The will's hung in probate court
It's a matter of time
before what was his
is mine, Roseanne

I ought to spit in your eye
You never even said he died
From now on I'm filling you in
Okay, let's try it again
but don't swing on me
If you do
I'll get you in your dreams

Step by step we walk the line
from Sixty-eighth to a Hundred and nine
Somewhere round Seventy-fifth
Roseanne starts looking ticked
You're gonna laugh at me
After I packed up
I turned in the key

Turned in the what? *That's what I did*
Roseanne you gotta be kidding
No, babe, we're out on the street
No shit, where do we eat?
On Amagamalin Street
At the Silver Snare
I got credit there

Ain't much but it's open late
Cheap and cheerful, grab a plate
Gimme a hammer, I'd crack this bun
CC Rider, what you done-done
you done-done
What you done-done
you done-done

Where will tonight end?
Pray for a new friend
Otherwise we ride the train
to Rockaway and back again
Far Rockaway
Far Rockaway
till the break of day

We could cop some cheap ice
Deal it cut twice
then head out of state
and wait for probate
I leave it to you
Roseanne
What do you wanta do?

Okay, we head for the coast
Out of New York, stop fighting ghosts
Hole up in the Mission, scratch for rent
For you, babe, I'd live in a tent
Spend every last cent
on roses and wine
Just give me the sign

. . . . .

S.F. setting
Otis Redding
Bay at sunset
What's that line of Frost?
Miles to go but I ain't lost
You're a Gypsy to me
I'll tell you what I see . . .

You'd look fine in a widow shawl
by candlelight with crystal ball
Good market in second sight
You know you look just right
Pull your hair back tight
Yeah, you got it in spades
Be queen of the trade

One thing I noticed today
people believe what you say
You read souls, what people feel
You know, we could make a steal
You got natural grace—
a Gypsy face
be a shame to waste

I believe your gift is real
and I know how to wheel and deal
You see through me, that's a fact
That's second sight, ain't no act
I know you can
Madam Roseanne
I want to be your man

. . . . .

Roseanne
where did the winter go?
Spring and summer, too
I'm feeling so down and blue

There's a customer at the door
Baby, why you looking so sore?
What do you mean it's insincere?
Tell 'em whatever they want to hear
Play it by ear

Cut the line about giving it up
We're starting to make bucks
Clients lining up at the door
What do you mean you feel like a whore?
Now what you say that for?

Why don't you dim the light?
Powder that black eye
Save the martyr routine
You sound like a broken machine
You better understand
a man has a right
to step out at night

You lie around reading swill
acting mentally ill
Where in the hell did you hide the wine?
Drank it yourself? That's real fine
Really first-rate

Look, I got you a date
Get yourself straight
. . . . .

Hello, Roseanne, I'm in New York
Appearance in probate court
Take care, I'll call when I can
'Course I love you, Madam Roseanne

Madam Roseanne, Madam Roseanne
Gypsy to me—Roseanne
Fall, winter, and spring
Two hearts with red wings
All those sweet thing
Gold hearts with bat wings . . .
Lining the dark part
Spring, summer, and fall—
I'll make that call
Fall, winter, and spring
She just lets it ring
She either isn't at home
or she's not alone . . .
I'm sure she's doing well
She's got something to sell
She's a Gypsy to me
Roseanne
I want to be your man
Madam Roseanne, Madam Roseanne
Roseanne—Gypsy to me . . .

AMAGAMALIN STREET

Chet and Murphy were the best of friends
When it come to Maggie the friendship ends
You can load up that gun but God help you, Chet
You can't pop all the ones Maggie ain't met yet

Once upon a time or two
Maggie came by man, what could I do?
Please understand I didn't make the move
If you knew what I know you might even approve

Hit the pavement and roll
Amagamalin Street
Try to make ends meet

It's only money, Murphy
What do you mean, Chet?
You may have yours but I ain't got mine yet
See that sign with three balls shaking?
Got everything of mine they thought was worth taking

Say, Chester, where'd you get that hat?
I found it at the laundromat
Say, you have good luck pretty nearly all the time!
I wouldn't say that but I do get mine

Hit the pavement and roll
Amagamalin Street
Try to make ends meet

Take Maggie and go
Got a feeling to roll
Wet my feet
On Amagamalin Street

Corner Potiphar Street and well . . .
There's a cozy place underneath the el
Where the touch of saint in the sinner can shine
Don't crowd that place 'cause it could be mine

Chet and Murphy were the best of friends
Ain't nothing doing but to make amends
One good pal is worth a crowd of folks
that don't cry at your bummers or laugh at your jokes

When walking . . . walking along
Amagamalin Street
Trying to make ends meet

Take Maggie and go, got a feeling to roll
Damn your soul—You got it under control
So take her and go—shake, rattle, and pray
It's the luck of the roll—they just lay that way

GYPSY PARLOR LIGHT

Whacked out on the corner
Pockets lined in gold
Gypsy parlor light
shining in the freezing cold

Cross my palm with silver
With makeup she'd be cute
Pay before you hear, she said
I'm gonna tell the truth

Gypsy parlor light . . .

Break it to me gently
She looked into my eyes
*I see a man who doesn't
listen to advice*

Just tell the future
I can figure what to do
*Well, you walked out on someone
who's better rid of you*

Gypsy parlor light . . .

Started sweating silver
She told me true
but I paid for the future
not yesterday's news

*Let me see your left hand
Now let me see your right
No, you ain't got a future
just a party every night*

Gypsy parlor light . . .

You can't mean that
You're telling me a lie

*No, I see the very hour
and the minute you die*

Look here, Gypsy woman
I don't want to know no more
She said: *Ain't no more to tell you*
as I stumbled out the door

Gypsy parlor light . . .

Took me a stroll down
Amagamalin Street
Tried to forget her,
she's a bummer and a cheat

I fell in with Murphy
Told him what went down
He said: *There ain't no Gypsy parlor
in this part of town*

Gypsy parlor light . . .

—I saw it with my eyes
I'll take you to the spot—
we retraced my footsteps
and found a vacant lot

Murphy, he was raised
in this very part of town
said *this lot, it was a rooming house
before they tore it down*

Gypsy parlor light . . .

*They put up seedy winos
and ladies of the street
As down-and-out a clientele
you'd never want to meet*

You must have had a vision
whatever it is worth
Time to change your action, pal
Get it down to earth

Gypsy parlor light . . .

I've had enough advice
to last me for a year
He said: *Yeah, whatever's right*
so we stopped and had a beer

Drunk by seven-thirty
looking for a friendly fight
I love a little party
and I love it every night

Gypsy parlor light . . .

Rolling home alone
as luck would have it took a right
where I should have took a left
Saw the Gypsy parlor light

Wasn't feeling any pain
Wasn't scared or anything
I just knocked upon the door
Hollered: *What's the future bring?*

Gypsy parlor light . . .

A wino on the steps
with eyes as red as port
Said: *You must be freezing, Chet*
Sit down and have a snort

That's exactly what I did
I drank the bottle down
He bummed a couple dollars
Said: *I'll see you around*

Gypsy parlor light . . .

Gypsy parlor door
opened with a creak
I come to find the day and hour
of which I heard you speak

I stared on her face
She wasn't pretty anymore
Looked half a century older
than she did the time before

Gypsy parlor light . . .

Cross my palm with silver
if you want to know your fate
—Here's a hundred-dollar bill, Gypsy
give it to me straight—

Your future's in that room
at the end of the hall
Here's the key, if you dare,
your fate is on the wall

Gypsy parlor light . . .

I saw nothing but the paper
on the wall, what did she mean?
Scabby yellow flowers in
a shabby city scene

The room started spinning
The rest is a blot
Woke up Sunday morning
sleeping in a vacant lot

Gypsy parlor light . . .

My head was real fuzzy
and my hands blue from chill
as I felt for my wallet
with the money from the will

Counted 10, 20, 30 40
50 dollars still
Strip of old wallpaper
but no hundred-dollar bill

Gypsy parlor light . . .

No one believes my story
They just look at me rude
Say: *What the hell's a strip
of old wallpaper prove?*

*What the hell's a strip
of old wallpaper prove?
Gypsy parlor light . . .
Gypsy parlor light . . .
Gypsy parlor light . . .
Gypsy parlor light . . .*

RAMBLING GHOST

I'm not an easy mark, I've seen too much
    much
Had money once, I was an easy touch
If I had a little less bone in my back
I'd beg for the things I lack
a smoke, a drink, a place to sack
I don't bum, I hustle my ride, it's a point
    of pride

Amagamalin Street
Amagamalin Street

Stand in back if you want my place in line
A life of pleasure alone and a worried mind
Three-day stubble and a cigarette cough
Honey, you're so pretty and soft
Where lights are bright and it's loud
I blend well with the crowd

Amagamalin Street
Amagamalin Street

I often wonder what happened to my Roseanne
Don't get me wrong, I don't really give a damn
She was a decent girl, hardly my style
We hooked up for a little while
I was good to her but she was a child
Set her up out west—no, thanks, though I did my best

Amagamalin Street

Whatever happened to Murphy and my Maggie, too
She was my kind of woman but, Lord, what *can* you do?
They might of got married, they were both uptight
but why raise apples when the peaches are ripe?
With luck I'll find a party tonight
Strange about that Gypsy parlor light

Amagamalin Street
Amagamalin Street
Out of thirteen people who come here,
    twenty-six stay
Half of them haunt the street, the rest hide
    away
They call me the Rambling Ghost
It's my pleasure to be your host
You buy the bottle and I'll drink a toast
to the kind of people you meet on
    Amagamalin Street
trying to beat the heat
Amagamalin Street
Trying to make ends meet
Amagamalin Street
Amagamalin Street

ITHACA

The Lady was born in Ithaca
twenty-three years ago
Wait until the sun shines
and the chariot swings low
Go ahead and hitch your line
in the time it takes to tell
Hold tight and ride it right
It'll always serve you well

You know, you keep coming back
in the wind of a dream or two
What could I do?

We met on Amagamalin Street
a year ago last night
She was with a friend of mine
who never treated anyone right
Being as much of a gentleman
as my Denver soul permits
I tipped the hat I later lost
and there was an end to it

But no, she kept coming back
in the wind of a dream or two
What could I do?

I saw my friend nearly every night
he was drinking himself insane
I once asked how the lady was
He couldn't recollect her name
Which might not seem so strange
if they didn't *live* together
That is, he lived off of her

His real home was the gutter
. . . What could I do?

I wasn't raised to rip off friends
I'm low, not out the bottom
Odd beginnings have common ends
ask the ones who brought 'em
It's not like he needed her
to save him from disaster
That's not exactly how it is
with a third-rate punch-drunk bastard

She kept coming back
On the wings of a dream
What could I do?
What could I do?

I had eyes for a full-time scene
but her words didn't fit my song
I understood that all out front
She never led me on
The truth is: Her crossed gray eyes
made it easy to do wrong
Thinking back I realize
I was doing it all along

The way she kept coming back
on the winds of a dream or two—
what could I do? What could I do?

(This song begins Part Two of "Amagamalin Street." The narration is now in the words of Murphy.)

DON'T BE DECEIVED

Hey, babe, look at you—
eight shades of black and blue
You look like you could use
someone to talk to

You know, me, I'm in a bind
since your man is a friend of mine
I know him as a son of a gun but
he's a son of a bitch with a woman

Don't be deceived
Don't be deceived

If I had a girl like you
I know what I'd do—
and I know, yes, I do
what I wouldn't do, too

I want to help but what can I do
unless he turns on me like he did on you
It's not a question of unconcern
To see what he's done makes me burn

Don't be deceived
Don't be deceived

I'll say it and I mean it, too,
next time he swings on you
don't you take it lying down
Honey, you just come around

You come back if it happens again
Don't feel you ain't got a friend
I'll take matters in my hands,
ethics of the road be damned

Don't be deceived
Don't be deceived

Hey, babe, look at you—
eight shades of black and blue
You look like you could use
someone to talk to

Don't be deceived
Don't be deceived
Don't be deceived

TAKING MAGGIE HOME

I'm taking Maggie home
She don't wanta stay
Walking out of here peaceful
Don't stand in our way

You had your chance
I didn't muscle in
But the way you treat this lady
is a shame and a sin

She came to me
Now I'm coming to you
She was yours, man
but that's all through

You got blood in your eye
but you know what I mean
You start swinging
every time you let off steam

Maggie's leaving you
I'm not dragging her off
If you make a move to stop her
it's gonna turn rough

She's had enough
but she's scared of your rage
Make like a book, Chet
and just turn the page

She's too good for you
Too good for me
Too good for both of us,
that's plain to see

You think you love her
but refuse to understand
she ain't your reflection—
she's a woman

I'm taking Maggie home
She don't wanta stay
We're walking out of here peaceful
Don't stand in our way
Don't stand in our way

OUT OF THE CITY

Take you out of the city
It's doing you no good
Get up and get out
Don't you think we should?

Cynicism is unbecoming
on a face sweet as yours
Underneath the makeup, baby
I can read the score

Out, out, out of the city
where violins are playing
Honky-Tonk of Love
Out, out, out of the city— for good

You done all kinds of things
you know you shouldn't do
Get out before it shows
like neon off of you

I done things I'd rather not
explain explicitly
You know what you have to do
to live here, let's break free

Out, out, out of the city
where violins are playing
Honky-Tonk of Love
Out, out, out of the city—for good

Out of the city—out of the city
Out, out, out of the city
where violins are screaming
Ain't no place for love
Out, out, out of the city for good

Get out before we blow apart
I'm not talking 'bout a lark

Chariot don't swing low here,
can't find no place to park

If you believe what I believe
and I've reason to believe you do
you'll come and go with me
You know damn well you would

Out, out, out of the city
where violins are playing
Honky-Tonk of Love
Out, out, out of the city— for good
Out of the city, out of the city . . .

Out, out, out of the city
where violins are screaming
Ain't no place for love
Out, out, out of the city for good

Out, out, out of the city
where violins are playing
Honky-Tonk of Love
Out, out, out of the city—for good

Out of the city, out of the city . . .

BETTER BAD LUCK

Broke-down '49 Ford by the side of the road
Hubcaps shining but it won't carry the load
Lucky we don't have anywhere special to go
Maybe we'll just settle down here, I don't know

Why don't we look at it philosophically
Coulda broke down in the Lincoln Tunnel halfway to Jersey
Instead of this fireplace Fall in the Catskill range
I believe we're on a run of better bad luck for a change

It feels like a holiday from jail
There's no way in the world out here to fail
All our stuff in the car, high hopes for a good clean break
from the life we left behind for true love's sake

Hey, babe, reach over and give me five
Hey, ain't it good to be alive?
Don't you get the feeling we've arrived?
A hundred and fifty miles from the nearest jive

Hey, ain't it good to be alive?

Might have to eat my words in an hour or two
When the sun hangs low in the heaven and the cold clear dew
begins collecting on the hood—the hood of our broke-down '49 Ford
reflecting the moon
I'll get to worrying then, but not too soon

Would you like to take over and pretend to drive?
Ain't it good—good to be alive?
Here in the fireplace Fall of the Catskill Range
I believe wc're on a run of better bad luck for a change
Hey, babe, ain't it good to be alive?
a hundred and fifty miles from the nearest jive?
Hey, ain't it good?
Hey, ain't it good?
Hey, ain't it good?

STREETWISE

You said—you said you love me
You said—you said you care
Now you—you don't say anything
You just sit there and stare

Streetwise
You never rock the boat
Streetwise
You know the way of the road
Streetwise
But can you survive
the test of fire and come out alive?

You never say you're sorry
You never say okay
You don't say—anything
You just look through me that way

Streetwise
You got a heart made of stone
Streetwise
Know how to go it alone
Streetwise
When you're down on your luck
just stick out your thumb and
flag down a truck

Just say count on me
Life could be so easy
Say you do or don't agree
but don't just sit there and be

so-so-so . . .
Streetwise
You've seen it all before
Streetwise
You know a door is a door
Streetwise
You just open it wide,

step into the street
and leave it all behind

You said you love me
and you said you care
Now you don't say anything
Just sit there and stare

Streetwise
Don't even rock the boat
So streetwise
Know the way of the road
Streetwise
But can you survive
the test of fire and come out alive?

Streetwise
You've seen it all before
Streetwise
You know a door is a door
Streetwise
just open it wide,
step into the street
and leave it all behind . . .
So streetwise!

FACE ME

Face me!
Don't make a sound
You got nothing to be scared of
I won't knock you around

I know you been making love
I think it's insane
How can you let him drag you down
then run to him again?

Face me!
Face me!

I'm not asking you to leave him for me
Lord knows I'm shot anyway
Still out fighting the long, long war
Ain't much else to say

I won't cross the street for your chances
resurrecting that bum
Damn these twisted romances
He'll beat you like a drum

Face me!
Face me!

There's a shot-out lamplight
way down along Amagamalin Street
One day he'll be lying beneath it
cut right off his feet

I won't be the one that does it
But I won't cry when he falls
His life don't mean nothing to me
Just drag you down is all

Face me!
Face me!

I just want you to face me
Why should you pretend it didn't go down?
I'm not your other man, remember
I won't knock you around

Yeah, of course I'm bitter as hell!
Got every right to be
I pray to God you find someone else
even if it isn't me

Face me!
Face me!

Got one more thing to say
Honey, you you can go or you can stay
Either way be straight with me
You know there's no other way

I'm sick of the whole damned scene
Get out if you've got a mind
I don't pretend to know what it means
but I'm not deaf, dumb, and blind

Face me!
Face me!

WHERE DID YOU GO?

Knock on the door
An echo returns
Where love flamed
emptiness burns
The streets are empty
The bars are closed
I take out a room
and I sleep in my clothes

Where did you go?
I want to know

Laying awake
in a strange part of town
Sky like slate
Rain patters down
Check-out time
believe it or not
Last buck for coffee
It's weak but it's hot

Where do I go?
I want to know
Where do I go?

The folks on the street
look weary and gray
Was it love gone wrong
done them that way?
My reflection in the window
has the face to say
I'm just another loser
on the street today

Where did you go?
I want to know

It went by so quick
all that remains
are variations
on the theme of pain
A fat crack of thunder
seems to call my name
I forget you a minute
ducking out of the rain

Where does it go?
I want to know
Oh, where did you go?
Where did you go?

13 ROSES

Got my right shoe on
Got my left shoe ready
Soon as I slip it on
I could turn and walk away
walk away . . .

Could cop an attitude
Take exception several ways
Truth is I misconstrued
the way some people play
The way they play . . .

Sunlight through a looking glass
somewhere in someone's past
13 long-stem roses
wave a long good-bye

Music from the street drifts up
A violinist in the dusk
drags the strings and makes them cry
You'll be mine—but not tonight
It isn't right

13 long-stem roses
wave a long good-bye

I heard about you long ago
from a sad case I used to know
Feels like we've met before
As though you grew up next door

He talked about your easy grace
you slender hands, your Gypsy face
The last word he spoke
I heard it clear
it was your name

Sunlight through a looking glass
somewhere in someone's past
13 long-stem roses
wave a long good-bye

13 long-stem roses wave a long good-bye
13 long-stem roses wave a long farewell
13 long-stem roses wave a long good-bye

Eagle Mall

INTRODUCTION

This saga was written in 1968–1969, a pet project of mine intended for setting and performance by the Grateful Dead. In retrospect, it was too ambitious a lyric project for practical consideration. The direction we took with *Workingman's Dead* was more to the point. However, the warm reception given by audiences to *Terrapin Station,* a similarly outré oeuvre concerning some of the same characters, shows that the boundaries of rock can be successfully stretched more than is commonly conceded—unless, of course, one is seeking a "hit," in which case more normative rules probably apply. *Eagle Mall* recounts the trials of a nomadic people and embraces the notion of eternal recurrence. The concluding parts of the reprise are intended to be sung simultaneously as a kind of "round."

JOHN SILVER

Oil my joints and tape my bone
It's time to walk again around the ring

For seven long years we marched
through the deserts of long-lost
John Silver, old buck, to the wheel plied he,
turn it down, 'round, under
where the Moon Pit glitters,
through the Valley of the Shadow ran he

No one knows how long we were gone,
time ain't reckoned that way
in the Moon Pit desolate world below
Come shoulder John's wheel
heave it up and around then
follow the trail till it cuts on down,
on down through the vision of a bright hot fire

Whoever can tell what things make a man?
John Silver, old buck, did the best you can
A mighty old giant from the dawn of time
he moved like a dancer through the pits of lime
in the nightmare castles of the lonely

I followed him out one dawn
and firmly stood my ground
Could of run if I wanted, but I didn't at all
Shoulder John's wheel, heave it up and around
then follow the trail till it cuts on down
Don't run, don't hide, don't reckon,
just wander on through

Old John plied the wheel,
like Silver was he,
drew a breath, wiped sweat,
grinned wide and bright, said:

Follow me down when the wheel draws tight
Down, I allow, in the shadowy pit
where he glistened like an angel
in the bright hot fire

With a voice like silken thunder
he'd sing of the world down under
tunes to chill your bones, set your eyes afire
while night passed over like a summer shower
when he sang away the dark and brought the dawn in

The old folks gather sometimes at night
when the desert stars are eyes of light
We talk of an evening when the moon is clear
about John Silver and the wheel of fear
How we marched single file through the bright hot fire

To the edge of the desert we came
To the land that had no name
John Silver turned back, to the desert retired
to gather the souls that were still untried
Untried by the vision of a bright hot fire

Gantree led the men
with Copper next in command
through the desert's heat, to the cool of night,
for days on edges where the sun burned bright
Bright as the silver-eye wheel drawn tight

For seven long years we marched
through the deserts of long-lost
John Silver, old buck, to the wheel plied he,
turn it down, 'round, under where the Moon Pit glitters
Through the Valley of the Shadow ran he

INVOCATION

Starlight
Starlight . . .
To the Eagle Palace with walls of water we came
Long had we chanted her name through our dreams
but the name disappeared when the dawn came

Quiet winter
Seasons flood by
Stand as you're able
The clock measures nothing
The sky is not space
is not sky
Here am I,
the Father
The Keeper of sight
and of records

COPPER

Copper grabbed a bridle, a waiting horse, and he did ride
Fast as anybody ever had been known to ride
The news was out in not more than an hour
all along the regions lying near around

The minions of the sun were sweet as apple wine to him
He laid his head by the shadow of a wayside inn
Mother of God, he didn't spend much time as a child
Didn't have much left to spend as a man

Racing like the sun 'cross the meadow of Belinda's dream
his heart was a nest in the bower of the forest green
His charge was the honor of the palaces of Valentine
and he cast no shadow when the sun hung in midstream

They said: *Take a message directly to the king*
Tell him the truth of this matter isn't what it seems
Instruct him some and then return to me
Our ship is rigged with sails of mist
and anxious for the sea

Racing like the sun 'cross the meadow of Belinda's dream,
his heart was a nest in the bower of the forest green
His charge was the honor of the palaces of Valentine
and he cast no shadow when the sun hung in midstream

Copper grabbed a bridle, a waiting horse, and he did ride
Fast as anybody had ever been known to ride
The news was out in not more than an hour
all along the regions lying near around

303

LAY OF THE RING

Josephus lately of the mountain wild,
seated before a desert fire,
Led the men to silence
while the fire told its tales
sketched in time the deeds of heroes
sketched in blood the trials of men

Where she lies in sandy wastes
the Sphinx observes the traces traced
Seven times 'round and seven times seven
around the driving wheel spins
Old beyond believing, beyond measure
Man and Lion, Bull and Eagle
observe the revolutions of the wheel

Barren O barren, O stretches of sand
reflected in water, no lay to the land
Ominous round of the *Uala Uala*
Silver reflected: a wheel a wheel

Raise the drinking horn
Pass the meat around
Brick by brick the wall evolves
Year by year the sun revolves
Age by age the ancient wheel
creaks and turns around

Oil my joints and tape my bones
It's time to walk again around the ring

Ring, Ring, the Ring soit quoi
Ring, Ring, the Ring soit quoi
Ring, Ring, the Ring soit quoi
Ring-a-levio the Golden Ring

From the gates of Numinor
to the walls of Valentine
It's seven cold dimensions
past the Mountains of the Moon

From the call of Chanticleer
to the ears of quick Reynard
lies a year of meadow
but the sound can travel clean

Raise the drinking horn
Pass the meat around
Brick by brick the wall evolves
Year by year the sun revolves
Age by age the ancient wheel
creaks and turns around

Let us play at madness, comrade
said the Devil to the Man
I'll drift a marker into time
and you go get it back again

A million years in time to wander
brought a smile to the lips of Man:
Send some token I know not of
clothed in legends whispered low of
Split me into many men
and we'll retrieve it how we can

The Eagle leaves the Land of Law
a silver chalice in his claw
The land will grow, the crops will flourish
Men will die and babes be born
and all the times we've had we'll have again

Raise the drinking horn
Pass the meat around
Brick by brick the wall evolves
Year by year the sun revolves
Age by age the ancient wheel
creaks and turns around

AT THE PASS

Gantree met the forces at the pass,
they ran away
He said: *Raise your tents this evening,*
let the piper earn his pay!
The whiskey rations doubled
though there's not a drop of beer,
for one man with a crossbow
can defend us from the rear

Copper walked the sentry
through the night until the day
but Gantree was too drunk
to hear his warning bugle play
Get up, get up, you rowdy cur
and lead your men to fray—
There's six for every one of us
a-coming up the way

Gantree raised his stick
and struck proud Copper 'cross the face
Mark your rank and mold your words
to that accordingly
A captain's faults are company
to no words but his own
So raise your voice and rouse your men,
there's battle to be done

"Arise, you men of women born
if to them you'd return
Clear your heads and grab your swords,
your lives now you must earn
The battle is upon us
and no man is sober here
The drunkest front and center
the rest fall to the rear"

Old Able stepped out from the ranks
and staggered to the fore
If drunker man than I be here,
he has not drunk down more
My brain burns with the fires of Hell,
my guts are passing sore
If any man contest me,
then I'll down a couple more

The piper played and the piper wailed,
the swords shone in the sun
The captain stepped past Able and said
You're drunker than all but one
And he led his men to battle
while the pipes they filled the sky
playing: *Whiskey, whiskey, whiskey*
and *Die, die, die*

EAGLE MALL

It wasn't that the matter was they hanged them
Copper and the captain side by side
The matter was the way they made us watch them
I guess a little piece of each man died

Captain killed the rear and forward watchmen
Copper cut the throats of those between
There wasn't any real thought of winning
That at least was plainly to be seen

It was all the matter begged to get off lightly
It was all the sound of pleading in the hall
It was over before we drew the cover
It was over by the time we faced the wall

In the nearest place they gather for the shadow
The sand has rolled across the Eagle Mall
Our banners, torn and tattered, lace the desert
The winter closes in upon the fall

The wind, it winds around the core of evening
The Eagle Mall is cold and oh, so quiet
Step into the center, you may touch it
where the crippled chalk has scribbled its *good-night*

The languages we spoke have been forgotten
The windows to the age are white as chalk
All the matters settled are as nothing
And all which was is like that which is not

Raise the drinking horn
Pass the meat around
Brick by brick the wall evolves
Year by year the sun revolves
Age by age the ancient wheel
creaks and turns around

Oil my joints and tape my bones
It's time to walk again around the ring
Ring—the Ring soit quoi
Ring-a-levio the Golden Ring

Often of a night I yearn to wander
as once I did when all my bones were whole
The desert's lovely, dark, and cool as orchids
The ghosts of old sing sweetly 'round my door:

Raise the drinking horn
Pass the meat around
Brick by brick the wall evolves
Year by year the sun revolves
Age by age the ancient wheel
creaks and turns around

I gave my love a mirror carved of starlight
I gave my love a ribbon edged in flame
My drinking horn lies shattered in the desert
My seeds are cast in places without name

The voices on the land obscure
the faces that dissolve
into the years

Raise the drinking horn
Pass the meat around
Brick by brick the wall evolves
Year by year the sun revolves
Age by age the ancient wheel
creaks and turns around

Oil my joints and tape my bones
it's time to walk again around the ring

Seven rings of silver
on his birthday in the sand

Ring around the charm-ed daisy
growing 'twixt the sea and land

Ring, Ring, the Ring soit quoi
Ring, Ring, the Ring soit quoi
Ring, Ring, the Ring soit quoi
Ring-a-levio the Golden Ring

Seven traces binding
all the sandy shore and land
to the charm-ed sleeping daisy
with the ring upon her hand

Ring, Ring, the Ring soit quoi
Ring, Ring, the Ring soit quoi

The Eagle leaves the Land of Law
A silver chalice in his claw
The land will grow, the crops will flourish
Men will die and babes be born
and all the times before we'll have again

Raise the drinking horn
Pass the meat around
Brick by brick the wall evolves
Year by year the sun revolves
Age by age the ancient wheel
creaks and turns around

For seven long years we marched
through the deserts of long-lost
John Silver, old buck, to the wheel plied he
turn it down 'round under where the Moon Pit glimmers,
through the Valley of the Shadow ran he

Ring, Ring, the Ring soit quoi
Ring, Ring, the Ring soit quoi
Ring, Ring, the Ring soit quoi
Ring-a-levio the Golden Ring

Oil my joints and tape my bones
It's time to walk again around the ring

T e r r a p i n   S t a t i o n

INTRODUCTION

I wrote *Terrapin,* Part One, at a single sitting in an unfurnished house with a picture window overlooking San Francisco Bay during a flamboyant lightning storm. I typed the first thing that came into my mind at the top of the page, the title: *Terrapin Station.*

Not knowing what it was to be about, I began my writing with an invocation to the muse and kept typing as the story began to unfold.

On the same day, driving to the city, Garcia was struck by a singular inspiration. He turned his car around and hurried home to set down some music that popped into his head, demanding immediate attention.

When we met the next day, I showed him the words and he said, "I've got the music." They dovetailed perfectly and *Terrapin* edged into this dimension.

Part One was for free. A good deal of Part Two, the essential idea, was contained in the first writing, but was too irregular to be easily set. I went through many approaches and versions over the years, having lost the original typescript, attempting to recapture the initial spark and place it in a lyric context.

"Jack O'Roses" and "Ivory Wheels/Rosewood Track" are examples of subsequent attempts to complete the cycle. They are included here as part of the suite since they *do* have pieces of the resolution within them, but they did not really satisfy the initial inspiration. I've omitted or changed a few lines from "Ivory Wheels/Rosewood Tracks," as I originally recorded it, feeling that they do not serve the rest of the work well.

Several years ago, I discovered the original typescript of *Terrapin Station* in one of the "files" of miscellaneous papers scooped off my desk and stashed away in trunks, at the completion of an album, to make way for new material. It is incorporated into this version, which I offer as reasonably complete.

LADY WITH A FAN

Let my inspiration flow
in token lines suggesting rhythm
that will not forsake me
till my tale is told and done

While the firelight's aglow
strange shadows in the flames will grow
till things we've never seen
will seem familiar

Shadows of a sailor forming
winds both foul and fair all swarm
down in Carlisle he loved a lady
many years ago

While the storyteller speaks
a door within the fire creaks
suddenly flies open
and a girl is standing there

Eyes alight with glowing hair
all that fancy paints as fair
she takes her fan and throws it
in the lion's den

"Which of you to gain me, tell
will risk uncertain pains of Hell?
I will not forgive you
if you will not take the chance"

The sailor gave at least a try
the soldier being much too wise
strategy was his strength
and not disaster

The sailor coming out again
the lady fairly leapt at him
that's how it stands today
you decide if he was wise

The storyteller makes no choice
soon you will not hear his voice
his job is to shed light
and not to master

Since the end is never told
we pay the teller off in gold
in hopes he will come back
but he cannot be bought or sold

TERRAPIN STATION

Inspiration move me brightly
light the song with sense and color,
hold away despair
More than this I will not ask
faced with mysteries dark and vast
statements just seem vain at last
some rise, some fall, some climb
to get to Terrapin

Counting stars by candlelight
all are dim but one is bright:
the spiral light of Venus
rising first and shining best,
From the northwest corner
of a brand-new crescent moon
crickets and cicadas sing
a rare and different tune

Terrapin Station
in the shadow of the moon
Terrapin Station
and I know we'll be there soon

Terrapin—I can't figure out
Terrapin—if it's an end or the beginning
Terrapin—but the train's got its brakes on
and the whistle is screaming: *Terrapin*

AT A SIDING

While you were gone
these spaces filled with darkness
The obvious was hidden
With nothing to believe in
the compass always points to Terrapin

The sullen wings of fortune beat like rain
You're back in Terrapin for good or ill again
For good or ill again

RETURN TO TERRAPIN

Up these steps beside me climb
to Terrapin and points sublime
Bereft of reason, faith and name
brokenhearted, blind, and lame

Slain by doubt, mistaken trust
Abandoned in the rain to rust
Torn to shreds by birds of prey,
Hostage to another day

Walk with me, talk with me
Tell me where we mean to go
and where we've been—
Crickets can say it and the wind:
Terrapin . . .

Trees in fields have
bees to tend them
Lilies have the wind
to bend them
Things have only
names we lend them
To the death
we will defend them

This light, so hazy—
cast by a new moon
through dense thought
to an ancient tune—
how pale the rays
as the light fades
through forest creepers
and clinging vines

but it does shine,
signature of the sun
cut in a thin slice,
a mere token of light
but it *does* shine—

failing only to be bright,
emblem of something
that shatters shadow
and all the dark defies . . .
Let the sun rise!

A long line to ride
A long black train
on a spiraling track
takes us back to Terrapin

IVORY WHEELS/ROSEWOOD TRACK

Ivory wheels on a rosewood track
Take us back again and again to Terrapin

Smokestack thunder—pay the ticket price,
Clock in the sky says quarter to twice
    —we roll again

Hello, good soldier, where you been?
Did you take the wrong way 'round to
    get to Terrapin?

Some for reasons great or small
Rise, climb, fall, to get to Terrapin

The demon's daughter used to lay for gin
In a shack way back on the skirts of the fens
    of Terrapin

The demon himself got drunk all night
Collapsed at the sunrise service—he was
    very tight

Captain Billy Lyon from Louisiana low
Used to chase a bayou girl through here
    named Peggy-o

Some say he died of love for Peggy-o
Others say it was the Devil himself laid
    Billy low

Some for reasons known but to them
Rise, climb, fall, to get to Terrapin

One-eyed sailor with a Chesire grin
That must be the Jack O' Roses bound
    for Terrapin

Chasing that lady-o through the bayou,
Swore to God in lightning storm he'd
    catch her, too

Fortune dealt him such a straight high hand
He saw no reason not to trust it more,
    and retrieved her fan

The lions looked up in surprise
But they backed right off when they saw
    the madness in his eyes

Venus rises from the sea
On the back of a mighty Terrapin with
    a coral fan

Throws that fan to the diamond beach
Always a little out of reach—but
    try again

Some for reasons great or small
Rise, climb, fall, to get to Terrapin

AND I KNOW YOU

Tonight I do not know my face
from one who looks the same
Am I late? Did we travel far?
Endless recognitions pour
like honey from a honey jar
turns and twists of love and loss
each one become the other
And I know you
and I know you know me, too
Yes, you do, you know me
I could almost swear you do

Let's get out of Terrapin Station
Symbol of our separation
Find out what we need to know
from gossip if it must be so—
Fill the blanks in as we go

I know you
Somehow I know you
Do we go together or leave alone
with brand-new shapes or broken bones?
I don't know how we chose before
but I could go with you
through that station door—
because I know you
and I know that you know me, too

JACK O' ROSES

What makes your sweet breast
    heave, my dear
your bright eyes fill with tears?
Did Jack O' Roses leave you here
these seven lonely years?

Had you fear he might be dead
unwept in some far land?
Or worse that love itself had fled
betrayed both heart and hand?

Jack O' Roses with a fan
East of Eden turned
built his castles in the sand
and all their bridges burned

Wait for him
Don't take no other
no demon lover
who'll be gone at dawn
Did you throw your fan
too far this time?
Well, well, well . . .
from the lion's den
to the morning star
to the gates of Hell!

The morning star rose into Hell
three days to shine on Moses
and from his solitary cell
to free the Jack O' Roses

He sprang to saddle like wind, I allow
for bridle strands of lightning
ride, ride, ride, though tempest howl
cruelly and most frightening

For at the dawn fair Terrapin
arose like revelation

The morning star reflected in
the windows of Terrapin Station

Terrapin
if anyone should ask of you who made this
    song
say the Jack O' Roses and all who played
    along
who rise, climb, fall to win
Terrapin

What have we to lose from love
except what lacks foundation
Words can only carve the space
we fill with expectation

The lion's den lies far behind
in visions of the damned
Jack O' Roses one more time:
My lady, here's your fan

Terrapin
let me rise, let me fall, let climb, let me
    crawl
but let me in
Accept this fan as a token of what I meant
    to do
for I really do love you

LEAVING TERRAPIN

Be careful how you speak of us
Take no one's name in vain
One day we will surely meet
in Terrapin again
As we lose our faith, we must,
guide us though insane
through this catalogue of souls
in search of grace and fame

If I have been a long time gone
It's not that love of you
has been forgot or ever cooled
or halved and broke in two
Outside major darkness
where the circle is complete
there is no fear that lovers born
will ever fail to meet

Was it you along beside me
who crawled out of the sea?
Who is that one sleeping
in the shadow of the tree?
Who is that beside her?
Is it who it seems to be?
Do not disturb their sleeping
Oh, true love, let them be

Too many times awakened,
they've just gone back to sleep
This time their dreams are peaceful
not tumultuous and deep
While starfish gather coral
beneath the foam and froth,
they offer hymns to Osiris
their hearts to Astoroth

Render us your blessing,
to multiply in kind

Send your mercy down among
the lame and halt and blind
Let us rest at ease and if
you die before we do
leave us words of love and peace
to stand instead of you

and some of the time
let the light shine
some of the time
let it shine

Although the stars have shifted,
we're not lost
The wind alone itself
decides our course
Seems such a long time
since we saw any land
but a seabird brought
this olive branch
and dropped it in my hand

All of this was sung before
and shall be sung again
Close your eyes
and hold your breath
and whisper: Terrapin
Orion sparkles overhead
but just a bit misplaced
eternity accounts for that
and your ever-youthful face

Inspiration move me right
Let sense and color guide me
Where other feet have stumbled
Lift me over lightly
Raise the weary voice and will
In strength to make a song
Not to make it perfect
But more nearly right than wrong

and some of the time
let the light shine
some of the time
let it shine

You look to me like starshine
on the foothills of the moon
Crickets make the rhythm
and cicadas play the tune
under a streaming sky
disguised as love alone
an ancient hunger wanders
like an ever-rolling stone

As long as it shines
by day or by night
as it *does* shine—
long as the light shines
in just enough dark
to be bright in
I know you
and you
know me, too

RECOGNITION

Trusting inspiration is
more often right than wrong
Raise again the drinking horn
And pass the meat around,

Light us, guide us
Raise us and lead us
Make certain our seed
has seed of its own
and seed of its seed
in turn, by the
grace of grace
who will shine
a good long time
and not fade away

Familiar stranger,
fates conjoined in
ways we cannot see,
I know you—come
with a lover's hope,
a lover's demand and
a lover's dream in mind
as long as the light shines,
as long as the words define
a space between you and I
to be measured in time,
until the day this station
closes forevermore
and no train runs from glory
to this godforsaken shore

Inspiration move me brightly
Light the song with sense and color
Hold away despair

More than this I will not ask,
faced with mysteries dark and vast—
statements just seem vain at last
Some climb, some fall, some rise
to get to Terrapin

Counting stars by candlelight
all are dim but one is bright:
the spiral light of Venus
rising first and shining best,
from the northwest corner
of a brand-new crescent moon
while crickets and cicadas sing
a rare and different tune
                              Terrapin Station

Flight of the Marie Helena

FIRST DAY

It rarely rains in dreams.
We hit all time lows and
very high estates, but rain—
no, it rarely does in dreams.

They say if you throw the lei of
golden blossoms far as you can and
they suspend in midair, then fly
back into your hand, you will return
to this blue island under blue clouds
rising from blue sea.
Blue above, blue below,
all is blue between.

Return to an isle where
wind whipped trees of teak
and mahogany clatter their
twigs like castanets.

With no thought of return
I press the golden lei into a book.
Later, the book may rise;
if not, perhaps the table.

The Marie Helena,
Our Lady Of the Tide,
largest raft the world has known,
rests upon the blue sand shore,
grounded in low ebb,
tethered by a silver cord
to a seaside carousel.

I am not a cloud. Feed me.
Press not into service one
who maketh wine of olives
to serve in porous cups.

Wind of fragrant lady's breath prefer,
though it rarely rains in dreams.
Carpets of interwoven
string quartets support us
as we take our leave and repair to sea
to follow the argument of the ocean;
to listen to the echo of a
great bell tolled beneath the waves
and toast the Marie Helena
Queen of the Blue Tide,
soon to sail!

Toast the Marie Helena with
a wink, a blink, a nod,
a bouquet of bougainvillea
and a hand me down guitar.

Empty that guitar of its
splendid oily rainbow.
pluck it out with patience,
the cleanest sort of vice.

Stage the bon voyage with
flagrant octarina;
lace the mask to your face
with living worms.

Strong hands unite!
Sign it into conscience!
Seal it with a fist;
for sail we will!

For each: a hammock strung
with sinew, bone and tendon;
soup and salt for each
and garnets in the gravy.

Place, law, climate and syntax
converge like wind to make the
Marie Helena thrash as
though she were a living thing.

A fragrance of excitement,
rising from the shoulders
of a deck hung with wistaria,
first inflames and then amazes.

Now the blessing
and the benediction.
Incense of carnation,
clove and oleander stream
from a swinging silver censer.

The eye of the tabernacle winks as the
chalice rises bolt upright on the altar,
shooting arrows of communion into
infidel and faithful hearts alike.

Accept the benediction of
a bent and bloody knee,
skinned on a gravel court
playing Hangman in rotation.

Shake a leg, blood lies still.
Clay is the rover.
There are rats in the scuppers!
Voulez vous couchez avec them?

The artist in the vein
has flustered reason.
The blood will not clot.
Worse, it will not flow.

From a seaside carousel,
a black robed figure waves;
a slow flick of the wrist
from a sleeve without a hand.

Toast the Marie Helena, pilgrim.
Bear your lacerations with resignation.
They will be healed within
the seven days we sail.

For a moment suspended,
wedged between two ticks of time,
caught between a sigh and inspiration,
the Marie Helena hesitates,
then with a shudder leaps
into the cheering foam.

The scent of orchids mingles with
the silk strings of a light guitar.
a blue-black cloud obscures
the seaside carousel. We sail!

In amniotic darkness
the Queen of the Blue Tide
sails beneath a counterpane of
self-reflecting mirrors.

The will of the wind be done!
We trust ourselves to the
providence of current and
the wisdom of the waves.

SECOND DAY

The dawn beside the lee
in morning aquaglimmer:
a clear prophetic seawalk
leads to afternoon.

A thousand different lines
can populate a song and
not disturb the sequence
of its melody.
Music hath no need of guardians.

Her sweet guitars,
harps, bells and calliopes
defend her.

Not the subject,
but the cadence;
less the cadence
than the tone . . .

Less subject, tone or beat
than angle of coincidence
seeking satisfaction of a
seventh sense of symmetry.

The Marie Helena glides upon
the bright white ocean of
our second day.
Everyone aboard her is
a stowaway. There were
no tickets for the passage.

Hanged in their lineaments,
sinister spinsters prowl
the foredeck and the aft
in search of lost angelicacies.

Thus do they paper their
implausibility with regret,
decline to elaborate.
Thin, wicked and celibate

Thus do they signify to me:
they remain in some sense
chained and offer constancy.
I'd not free them for the world.

They will scrub the deck for secrets;
discover blood drops and hasty
crumpled notes of secret love.
They will find small things of value
which they will not return.
God bless them.

Bell tower, peal forth.
Awaken all sleeping souls.
Shovel the master from
ashes, an approving flame.

The more the eyelids lower
the more an internal visor
opens on a vast
mechanical vista.

Words of emerald
shine beneath a
slow flowing sea with
light sighs and laughter.

What was it we feared when
setting forth to sail upon
this cheerful raft upon
this sweet and glossy sea?

Relax! Fear is endless
but here—oh, here is
time for music, for philosophy,
for poetry and even love!

Here is time for recognition,
reunion and recompense.
We will sail unto
whatever port the winds prepare.

Ah, blessed second day!
Two smiling dolphins breast our wake.
Lost from sight, our shore becomes
the lost blue peaks of memory.

INTERLUDE

An almighty knock
shatters the placid waves.
The sea becomes the sky
full of foaming flame!

Veins of the waves
bulge till they burst
and turn the sea to blood.
. . . . .
A raft has no fore or aft,
the Marie Helena has no sail.
Hell's own violin and Bacchanal
upon the southdeck wail;

"This is my creation!"
cries the thunder.
"I am pleased!
Now mop it up!"

To be done! To be done!
And then, under a swell,
sat down forcibly and
lectured by a cloud.

As I rolled to St. Alair,
the cloud declared,
I met a crippled king
with four fleshless hounds
leashed by seven chains.

A queen had he on the right arm
and three queens on his left.
Each queen had seven tongues,
each tongue of two opinions.

He combed the twelve hairs of his beard
with a currycomb of glass—
Ten tines had it on a time
but four, alas, are broken.

God above and Christ below,
counting the king, the queens,
hounds, chains and all
the several other things
how come
it rarely rains
in dreams?
It is because
there is no need.

There are dreams in which
other dreams are mentioned,
contiguous in symmetry, but,
in dreams, it very rarely rains.

THIRD DAY

Who kept the watch that
endured the night?
The watch from which
we woke from stormless slumber/
into the confectionery of
a gladsome dawn?

Who saw that the hour is
never the hour apparent,
awaited a history of history
from the hall of elucidation?

The first day held questions,
the second day posed riddles—
Today smacks of mystery.
Let us question one another!

Inside my fists a
theater of the dark;
throbbing to the lovely
lady without mercy.

I came to question her, how
comes she to question me?
All is coincidence!
One thing begets another.

Ah! But I itch and I
grow hateful for an hour,
my language composed of
noun, verb and nudity.

Slam the visor on this
small change arcade.
Open it upon
a rolling sea.

From a sea song foaming
with slashing brine;
from a sunbeam springs
a horse with tangled mane.

Hands across the sky reach
meeting without touching.
Feet beneath the sea stroll
on carpets of anemone.

The sky spills from its
dressing gown of cloud
where seven pointed starfish soar
on silent wings.

From a midday moon
there hangs a ballerina
twirling slowly by her teeth:
she is my witness.

She gains the handrail,
gently slides like butter
trailing down a sunwarmed
deck, pat by pat.

Is it she who watched
the storm kick out the jambs,
the ghost of her for whom this
craft is named "Marie Helene"?

How came we to the sea?
Who bid us come?
There is not a sailor in our midst.
Not one among us.

There are sunsets, stars
and omens to be figured;
winds that promise
ever greater fury.

Without Captain, crew or
lore, we are
captives of the tide.

It is better not to
recognize this plight.

It is better to
wear seaweed socks
than thrust a melon in
your brother's ear.

Tenderhearted ladies toss
wildflowers from the lookout,
out, out into a sunny flare
of glaring trumpets.

Before you cough,
take your hat off. Diamonds?
Diamonds were nothing.
We used to swallow them.

We shall be increased.
In spite of cadaverous
laughter, it stands
to reason. We provide.

Bless the
sailors and
the girls
who bite them.

These limits I defend.
Why overstep them?

They are where they are instead
of sails for the Marie Helena,

We will slime our horns
with the balm of Gilead,
clink skulls and drink,
deeply, one another's health.

A raging teardrop
in a timid fire,
completely minconstrued
and glad to be so.

You know best,
consorts of kings,
how little comfort
are Forget–Me–Nots.

Once.
Oh, once!
And then
no more.

Had I
dreamt of rain.
It would seem
an unusual thing.

Strike the visor on
this day of mystery.
Open it inside
the realms of sleep.

I fall until I feel I
must explode
with spray of salt spreading
ivory on the porthole.

FOURTH DAY

The fourth day dawns at midnight.
What should have been the moon
whirls like a scimitar swung round the
turban of some blood-drenched Saracen
beheading stars.

Question on the first day,
then riddles giving way to
mystery on the third;
today commences with apocalypse.

A shrill high fiddle note presides.
Transported to high ecstasy,
our fire-breathing eyes pour
music back into the violin.

Then saith God, "Call
you son Loammi meaning:
Ye are not my people.
I will not be your god. (Hosea I:IX)

"You shall abide many days
without a prince, a king,
a sacrifice, an image,
an *ephod* or a *teraphim*. (III:IV)

"Blood toucheth blood,
let the land mourn.
Thou shalt be
no priest to me." (IV:II,III,VI)

What? no *teraphim?*

Supplication seems inadequate.
It is too late for sacrifice.
Perhaps some sort of bribe
is apropos.

Tossing my wristwatch
into the snapping sea,
my timepiece is returned by an
indignant wave, rewound.

The soft hand of one
who is not, but almost,
present begins to stir
my hair with breezes.
. . . . .
Three more days of this,
a soft wind whispers,
the poison will subside.
The Marie Helena and
her ocean will provide.

A raft cannot ship water.
The Marie Helena will not drown.
It may float, becalm or spin
but it will never sink.

Those not disposed to vision gather
on the west deck, trade yarns and speak
of remarkable spitballs, delivered
with a touch of fire.

I go among them and speak
of innings, runs and scores.
We will speak of "going back for
a long one" and derive some
simple creature comfort therefrom.

Slam down the visor!
The moon becomes again a moon
of gentle incandescence
over the smooth, lapping swells.
The lion of the ocean sleeps.

INTERLUDE

True dawn.
Sea and sky, then
sky and sea,
fleck, foam, wave—
luminous blue rose.

An island lies
off stern—inviting.
Ah! If we could only
swing the Marie Helena!

But no, we are engaged to
ride the mighty raft where
wind and wave command!
Mark it on the map and wave farewell.

The perfume of its trees
ride on the breeze which
gently, firmly, sadly
bars our entry.
. . . . .
A very blue island
beneath blue clouds
against blue sky
rising from blue sea.

It is not a dream.
Ah no, it is another thing.
It is a sunlit vision
seen through rain.

FIFTH DAY

The fifth day: thunder without rain.
A small skull carved of
ivory sits, right profile,
in an unlit candelabra.

Yesterday, a determined smile carried
one corner of the sky clenched
between ragged teeth:
The sky which is a sheet.

Today a docile banner flaps
in half a breeze.
A pipe is clenched between
my teeth unlit.

Yesterday a velvet gloved claw bore
a cupful of the sky
in a milkwhite vase:
The sky which is a drop of blood.

Today I poured my tin cup of
salty soup into the sea
but not as a libation.
I had no taste for it.

Yesterday, a girl with lips of amber
printed a yellow kiss upon
a rounded ring of sky:
The sky which is my mouth.

Today, a lump of anthracite
hangs in a double dark sky;
the sky below, the sky above.
and in between: the sea.

Yesterday, with stool and milking pail,
I sat beneath the Mother Unicorn
with hands of storm
attempting to milk the sky.

Today nothing amazes or perplexes.
It is all too weary to perplex.
It only cauterizes or infects.

All which was professed a joy
becomes a present bore, in light of
one objection: I have
seen this all before!

Such redundancy calls
for brass, flute, woodwind
and sweet, resounding lips
to play them.   (interlude)

Oh, but the song is the same song
sung to the same tune once too often.
The answers to our questions have
proved less than entertaining.

A ride of a week and one week only.
Each day's sun ascends behind
a different deck.
Is this a circle that we sail?

We are reduced to ritual.
We have burned our graven images
for fuel. We find no significance
in numbers or the alphabet.

I look to the darkening sky and
see no constellations; only
slowly spinning stars
without cohesion.

From the southeast cusp of Leo pours
the realm of galaxies.
That is where you look
to look far, far away.
What begins with music
will end with music.

Between the music are
a number of things which
have to do with music
lacking only melody.

It is time for a midnight snack/of oranges, rosewater and
lavender pretzels made of china/which snap between your teeth.

SIXTH DAY

I thought of a colored pencil.
I thought it with soft blue lead.
I thought your picture, used the
flat side of the lead to shade.

I penciled in the sky and made
clouds with a kneaded eraser.
You will be my masterpiece, I
will sketch you from every angle.

Six dolphins circle round
the Marie Helena; one for
every day we've been at sea.
What profit reputation?

White cloud stallions dash
in unnemphatic rhythm
bright as any tinsel in the
chocolate dust of a red wind.

Four emphatic trumpets blare,
why be dismayed?
Without music we are prey to
the strange arms of reason.

Absolution, reconstruction,
resolution and forgiveness
pour from the brass bells
with a scent of lemon bloom.

Glad to be forgotten, I go
climbing in among the
reconstituted constellations
searching for a certain star.

Come shining from the afterdeck,
sweet echo of the singer.
Cello, lay your ecstasy
like leagues of spongy moss.

Emotions of the heart
must be surprised—
they languish for attention,
are shy.

I closed my eyes last night
but did not dream.
At dawn . . . gently, gently,
a patter of rain.
Silence has left a film of
satisfaction, paper thin,
upon the transparent ocean,
oh, but not upon my heart!

Instead I turn the capstan
to the squalid, squalid lee.
North by North or South by South
upon, beneath, between the sable sky.

In this way shall all
hearts be protected:
a tight membrane dispensing
merriment and absolution.

Again, a light rain. The
sea devours these clouds.
Storms are its meat; our hearts
will do for wine.

Consider how rigidly
the sky is painted.
How we wear it on our head
like a slowly spinning hat.

The Marie Helena speeds along
in a sleek current. A new
moon on the horizon casts
no hint of glare.

The shower is passed.
The sky is clear: Preserpe,
whose invisibility signals rain,
is discerned but not quite seen.

An absence of a dream of rain.
Six days at sea, much has been scuttled.
What, here at the end, seems
worthwhile to have brought aboard?

A few things seem certain.
Some scales, some equations.
Smaller matter the particular music
or the mathematics forced from them.

Or invert and it is
all the matter; all
the matter which
scarcely ever was.

Now one way,
now another.
Both, and others,/however pure.

Clay and cloud.
Cloud and clay.
Cloud and clay.

Leonardos have lept from
flaming towers for you, with
no suggestion or remotest
promise of fidelity.

Gilded to the lily,
you proudly plunge your hand
into the hive and scoop
the honey to your mouth.

This clear, transparent honey
has no flavor.
Should the Marie Helena
sail another week? Ah,
no—is is forbidden
by edict.

Tonight we swing into our hammocks
determined not to dream.
The warmth we seek from bodies
eludes us. Our bones are leather.

Tone by tone the midnight bell
beats twelve bright claps of
sweet forgiveness in these ears
of ears this night of nights.

SEVENTH DAY

Today a cratered rainbow
ascends with ragged beam
from a cup of morning coffee
into later afternoon.

The day is spent preparing
for a secular advent which
may well fall shy of
advertised proportions.

Seven days a-sail or a-spin,
however traveled, not at last
the world lies uncreate,
transparent to the core.

The vacation, hardly begun,
is over now. As the axis
of our fantasy dissolves,
we slowly wave in rhythm.

Waving at a passing raft
where reflections of ourselves
wave back a tear-stained flag
hung from a rope of onions.

Waving to the flippers of
seven silver silkies who
have tracked our wake all day,
now going separate ways.

Waving to children with gold
eyes upon a seaside carousel
who pursue one another in
stationary joy with screams of laughter.

Waving at a superior one-step epoxy,
good for bonding stainless steel to water.
Good for gluing the shoreline to the sea.

Waving at an Italian
organ-grinder on a skip.
His ape returns our wave
with his glass-beaded cap.

Waving at a public nuisance
spraypainting the rainbow and
to sea gulls circling counter to the
spinning wake of the Marie Helena.

Waving to a dark steamer,
dim even by unclouded sun.
Something waves back, or
perhaps it is a curtain.
Waving to the crucified
who lifts a finger in reply.
Waving to a blue, blue island which
was once our heart's desire.

Waving to a solitary gunman,
whose eye, magnified, winks
from the crosshair sight
trained in our midst.

Waving to an inflatable giraffe
bearing a poet in beret and shades
reciting, beating holy hell
out of a conga drum.

Waving to a foiled villain,
cloak and top hat streaming,
hissing as he twirls the points
of his elaborate mustache.

Waving, waving, waving
at a lei of golden blossoms
suspended in midair,
poised in indecision.

When we'd finished waving,
we danced to the creak of
an iron gate; danced to the clank
of the lid upon a boiling kettle.

We danced to the squeek of
chalk upon a blackboard,
breathing the sweet powder
of pounded erasers.

We danced to the whistle of
a carpenter stripping paint
and to the horns and sirens
of a falsified alarm.

We danced to the deep groan
of shifting continental plates
and to the muffled notes of
a jukebox in a hurricane.

We danced to the whine
of a dentist's drill and
the crunch of steps in
fresh powdery snow.

We danced to the howl of
a spook from out of a watery grave
and to the slither of its
slimy seaweed chains.

We danced in white and
scarlet ephods
on the ashes of our *teraphim*.

We danced to the rippling cadence
of a thousand-string guitar;
the deck awash in music, with
treble clefs of foam conducting.

We danced to the keen whine
of selective devastation, to a
world innocent of roses groaning/beneath
     a deep bowed
bass

We danced to the lullaby wail
of one almost but never quite
entirely present whom we have
loved but cannot fathom.

We danced upon logs of teak,
mahogany, ironwood and ebony.
The visor of the sky opened at perihelion
spreading to each horizon.

And when we'd finished dancing,
we broke down and wept.

We wept for crimson laces
in green leather boots.
We wept at a full ketch
of sardines and at the
pipe smoke of three fishermen
in animated conversation.

We wept because it so
rarely rains in dreams.
Our tears were fat, warm
and blue by reflected sky.

We wept for a three bar
jackpot in a ten cent
one-armed bandit spitting
dimes and ringing bells.

We wept forlorn, for long,
forever; caught our tears
in tiny crystal bottles
with blue glass stopples.

As we continued weeping,
our raft began to spin,
faster, faster, blurring like
a pinwheel in a hurricane.
We hold, we slip, we slide
as the Marie Helena
discharges passengers by
centripetal force.

Good-bye! we cry to one another.
Forgive these imperfections,
these tears of self-pity and
these infinite regressions.

Some hold hands, some fly
off separately, some by
fours and threes to the
place in which they land.

Some land in a haystack
in midsummer Somerset.
Some land in boxcars
rattling through the Klondike.

Some land in covered wagons
moving west, some land in
a borax mine admist the
clatter of mule teams.

Some fall down chimneys
on Christmas eve,
brush the soot from
scarlet suits and chuckle.

Some fall breathless onto
a seaside carousel
among the gold-eyed children
chasing one another endlessly.

Some fall on the desert
and crawl across the sand
into a promising mirage
that speaks of water.

Some, or none, or is it one
land upon a blue island. Beneath
white clouds against blue sky
rising from blue sea.

After a week's unfolding
many things have changed.
It is time now to
change them back again.

It is still true, in spite of
the flight of the Marie Helena,
still true, that it rarely,
very rarely, rains in dreams.

DISCOGRAPHY

When I have collaborated on songs most often the music was written by Jerry Garcia, generally listed in the credits as JG.

Other songs were written with Ron McKernan, Phil Lesh, Robert Weir, Bill Kreutzman, Mickey Hart, John Dawson, Keith Godchaux, Kevin Morgenstern, John Kahn, Barry Melton, David Freiberg, and Richard McNeese.

All Songs © Ice Nine Publishing Company unless otherwise indicated.

Collaborations with Jerry Garcia are indicated by initials due to their frequency. If no co-credit is listed, words and music are by Robert Hunter. Grateful Dead albums are indicated by roman type, all others by *italics*.

ANTHEM OF THE SUN—1968
  Alligator—lyrics: Hunter/McKernan;
    music: McKernan/Lesh
AOXOMOXOA—1969
  Saint Stephen—Garcia/Lesh
  Dupree's Diamond Blues—JG
  Rosemary—JG
  Doin' That Rag—JG
  Mountains of the Moon—JG
  China Cat Sunflower—JG
  What's Become of the Baby?—JG
  Cosmic Charley—JG
LIVE DEAD—1969
  Dark Star—Garcia/Lesh/Weir/Kreutzman/
    Hart
  The Eleven—Lesh
WORKINGMAN'S DEAD—1970
  Uncle John's Band—JG
  High Time—JG
  Dire Wolf—JG
  New Speedway Boogie—JG
  Cumberland Blues—Garcia/Lesh
  Black Peter—JG
  Easy Wind—Hunter
  Casey Jones—JG
AMERICAN BEAUTY—1970
  Box of Rain—Lesh
  Friend of the Devil—Garcia/Dawson/
    Nelson

Sugar Magnolia—Weir (lyrics: Hunter/
    Weir)
Sunshine Daydream—Weir
Candyman—JG
Ripple—JG
Broke-down Palace—JG
Till the Morning Comes—JG
Attics of My Life—JG
Truckin'—Garcia/Lesh/Weir
GRATEFUL DEAD (LIVE)—1971
  Bertha—JG
  Playing in the Band—Weir/Hart
  Wharf Rat—JG
EUROPE '72—1972
  He's Gone—JG
  Jack Straw—Weir
  Brown-eyed Women—JG
  Ramble on, Rose—JG
  Mister Charlie—McKernan
  Tennessee Jed—JG
GARCIA (*GARCIA SOLO*)—1972
  Deal—JG
  Bird Song—JG
  Sugaree—JG
  Loser—JG
  To Lay Me Down—JG
  The Wheel—JG
ACE (*WEIR SOLO*)—1972
  Greatest Story Ever Told—Weir/Hart

TALES OF THE GREAT RUM RUNNERS (*HUNTER SOLO*)—1973
- Lady Simplicity
- That Train
- I Heard You Singing—Freiberg
- Rum Runners
- Children's Lament
- Maybe She's a Bluebird
- Boys in the Barroom
- It Must Have Been the Roses
- Arizona Lightning
- Standing at Your Door
- Mad—Hart
- Keys to the Rain

WAKE OF THE FLOOD—1973
- Mississippi Half-step Uptown Toodeloo—JG
- Let Me Sing Your Blues Away—Godchaux
- Row, Jimmy—JG
- Stella Blue—JG
- Here Comes Sunshine—JG
- Eyes of the World—JG

FROM THE MARS HOTEL—1974
- U.S. Blues—JG
- China Doll—JG
- Loose Lucy—JG
- Scarlet Begonias—JG
- Ship of Fools—JG

TIGER ROSE (*HUNTER SOLO*)—1974
- Ariel—Hart
- Over the Hills
- One Thing to Try
- Tiger Rose
- Last Flash of Rock and Roll
- Cruel White Water
- Dance a Hole
- Wild Bill
- Rose of Sharon
- Yellow Moon

COMPLIMENTS OF GARCIA (*GARCIA SOLO*)—1974
- Midnight Town—Kahn

BLUES FOR ALLAH—1975
- Blues for Allah—JG

Crazy Fingers—JG
Franklin's Tower—JG/Kreutzman
Help on the Way—JG

REFLECTIONS (*GARCIA SOLO*)—1976
- Might as Well—JG
- Mission in the Rain—JG
- They Love Each Other—JG
- Comes a Time—JG

TERRAPIN STATION—1977
- Lady with a Fan—JG
- Terrapin Station—JG
- Terrapin—JG
- At a Siding—Hart

SHAKEDOWN STREET—1978
- France—Weir
- Shakedown Street—JG
- Fire on the Mountain—Hart
- Staggerlee—JG
- If I Had the World to Give—JG

CATS UNDER THE STARS (*GARCIA SOLO*)—1978
- Cats under the Stars—JG
- Gomorrah—JG
- Love in the Afternoon—Kahn
- Palm Sunday—JG
- Reuben and Cherise—JG
- Rhapsody in Red—JG

ALLIGATOR MOON (*HUNTER W/COMFORT—UNRELEASED*)—1978
- Mesa Linda
- Domino, Cigarette, and Melina—Morgenstern
- Domino—Morgenstern
- Blue Note—McNeese
- New East St. Louis Blue—McNeese
- Cigarette—McNeese
- She Gives Me Love
- Drunkard's Carol
- Hooker's Ball
- Jesse James—Melton
- Promontory Rider

JACK O' ROSES (*HUNTER SOLO*)—1979
- Book of Daniel—Freiberg
- Ivory Wheels/Rosewood Track—JG

Jack O' Roses—JG
Prodigal Town
Talking Money Tree
GO TO HEAVEN—1980
    Alabama Getaway—JG
    Althea—JG
PROMONTORY RIDER (*HUNTER RETROSPECTIVE ALBUM*)—1982
    Touch of Darkness
RUN FOR THE ROSES (*GARCIA SOLO*)—1983
    Run for the Roses—JG
    Valerie—JG
    Leave the Little Girl Alone—JG
    Midnight Getaway—JG
AMAGAMALIN STREET (*HUNTER SOLO*)—1984
    Roseanne
    Amagamalin Street
    Gypsy Parlor Light
    Rambling Ghost
    Ithaca
    Don't Be Deceived
    Taking Maggie Home
    Out of the City
    Better Bad Luck
    Streetwise
    Face Me
    Where Did You Go?
    13 Roses
ROCK COLUMBIA (*HUNTER SOLO*)—1984
    Eva
    End of the Road
    I Never See You

Aim at the Heart
Kick It on Down
What'll You Raise?
Who, Baby, Who?
Rock Columbia
LIVE '85 (*HUNTER SOLO ACOUSTIC*)—1985
    Sweet Little Wheels
IN THE DARK—1987
    Touch of Grey—JG
    When Push Comes to Shove—JG
    West L.A. Fadeaway—JG
    Black Muddy River—JG
LIBERTY (*HUNTER SOLO*)—1987
    Liberty
    Cry Down the Years
    Bone Alley
    Black Shamrock
    The Song Goes On
    Do Deny
    Worried Song
    Come and Get It
    When a Man Loves a Woman
DOWN IN THE GROOVE (*BOB DYLAN ALBUM*)—1988
    Silvio—Dylan
    Ugliest Girl in the World—Dylan
    (music for both songs © *Special Rider Music 1988*)
BUILT TO LAST—1989
    Foolish Heart—JG
    Built to Last—JG
    Standing on the Moon—JG

OTHER SONGS

. . . tunes recorded and/or performed but not released or left lying around or forgotten or simply not belonging to any of the above categories . . . lyrics marked with an asterisk (★) are from my performing repertoire but are not recorded . . .

L'Alhambra—Hart
Believe It or Not—JG
Boll Weevil Rag★
Born Sidestepper

Chingo!
Circulate the Rhythm
Come to Life—Steve Schuster
Cry in the Night

Dinosaur★
Eagle Mall:—1968
  John Silver
  Invocation
  Copper
  Lay of the Ring
  At the Pass
  Eagle Mall/Reprise
Elijah
Fair to Even Odds
Four White Horses
A Glass of Wine at the End of Time
Golden Stairs
The Handyman's Rhyme
Hollywood Cantata
Holy Brooklyn Crown
In a Love Dream
Independence Day★
It★
It's Only Music
Jacob Baum
Just Another Train
Keep the Watch
Keep Your Day Job—JG
Lay of the Sunflower
Lazy Tiger Rag★
Little Foxes
Lovin' Spoonful #9
Mason's Children—Weir/Lesh/Garcia
Miralda★

Molly Dee—Hart★
Must Be the Moon
No Place Here
Northeast by West
Only the Strange Remain—Hart
Only to Believe★
Parcel of Doom
Pieces of Eight
Red Car
Reelin' and A-Pitchin'★
Reno Roll
Roadhog
Shiny Blue Sea
Slack String Quartet★
Terrapin: additional material (1976–1989)
  Return to Terrapin
  And I Know You
  Sanctuary
  Leaving Terrapin
  Recognition
Testify
Tin Crown Blue
Tioga Pass
Tough Changes—Weir
Wheels that Spin
When the Lights Went Out
Willy Morris
Willy Poor Boy
Woodshed Time